how to garden

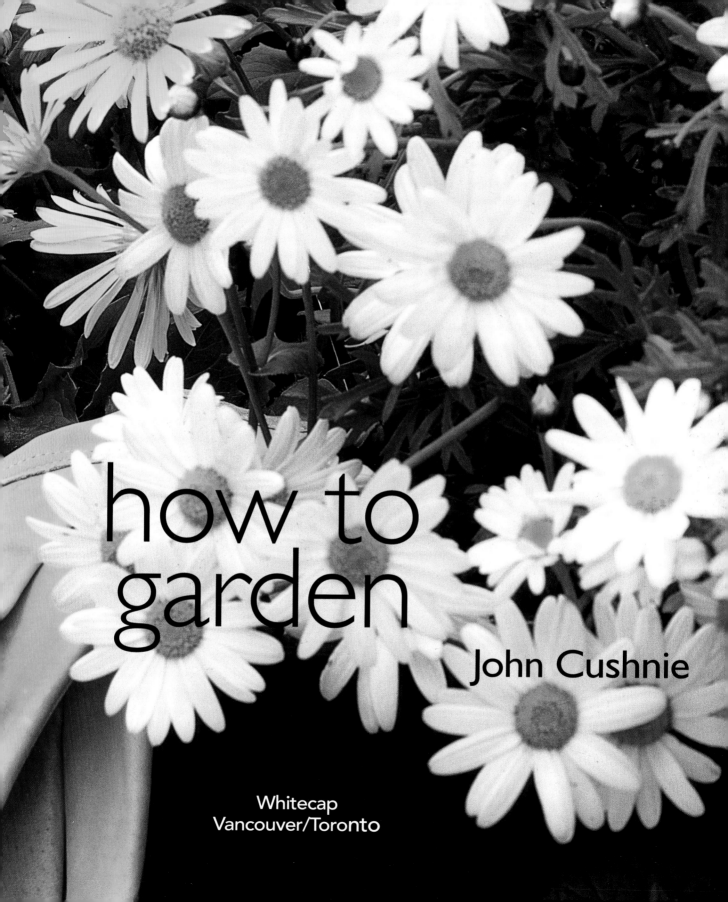

how to
garden

John Cushnie

Whitecap
Vancouver/Toronto

To Richard & Aisling
a couple of potential gardeners

This edition published in Canada by Whitecap Books
351 Lynn Avenue,
North Vancouver,
BC V7J 2C4

First published in 2001 by Kyle Cathie Limited

1-55285-242-3

© 2001 by John Cushnie
Photographs © 2001 by Steven Wooster
See also other copyright acknowledgements on page 192

Special photography by Steven Wooster
Project editor: Caroline Taggart
Text editors: Charlie Ryrie and Sharon Amos
Designed by Robert Updegraff • Illustrations by Elizabeth Kay
Production by Lorraine Baird and Sha Huxtable

John Cushnie is hereby identified as the author of this work in accordance with Section 77
of the Copyright, Designs and Patents Act 1988.

Printed in Singapore by Tien Wah Press

contents

A garden doesn't happen overnight, but it is worth waiting for. After all your hard work, you will have a very personal place to sit and relax.

introduction

There is a difference between new gardeners and people who have new gardens. This book is written primarily for the former, whose gardens may or may not be new. You may have some experience, gleaned from helping in your parents' garden when younger, but more likely the concept of gardening will be a bit of a mystery, perhaps laced with a dash of apprehension or even a full measure of apathy. But if, for whatever reason, you find yourself the owner of a garden, you need to learn how to look after it and turn it into a source of delight rather than a burden.

There are many ways to become a gardener, some more painful than others. If you are serious about it, going to horticultural college or gardening evening classes is admirable. Reading gardening books and magazines, watching television programs and getting tips from the radio are all helpful; joining a local garden club will introduce you to enthusiasts and enable you to pick their brains. One great way to get inspiration is to visit as many different gardens, large and small, as you can, making notes of ideas that might work in your garden and learning the names of plants that appeal to you.

But none of these is a substitute for getting out there in the garden, getting your hands dirty and setting about making plants grow. To do that successfully, you have to know the basics. The aim of this book is to teach you those basics – the rudiments of keeping your soil fertile and your plants healthy, of getting rid of weeds and minimizing pest attacks, of cutting a lawn and trimming a hedge – with just enough neat-and-tidiness to keep your neighbors happy, but without the whole thing becoming a millstone hanging over every weekend. It will also give you ideas for simple but successful plantings; for creating something you've always longed for like a cottage garden or your own patch of woodland; and for what to do with that dark boggy patch by the back fence.

Planting can be color coordinated, as with the sea thrift, pansy 'Red Blotch,' and pink forget-me-nots opposite; or an abundance of different hues complementing existing features, above.

You can start to garden at any age and the younger the better, because once you get the hang of it, you will love it and wish you had taken it up earlier. It is also an advantage if you are fit enough for the donkey work, because there is bound to be some of that. Healthwise, gardening is one of the best hobbies, bringing lots of exercise, fresh air, and the satisfaction of seeing plants maturing. People claim that it is therapeutic, but don't get too laid back about that – gardening can be pretty frustrating at times, most often because the weather is not always what you wanted or expected.

In the meantime, while these encouraging words are being written and read, the weeds are growing like crazy and the grass is growing like weeds, so I had better get on with some ways to garden.

Where do you start? There is no need for lots of paperwork, but in order to work toward your ideal garden, you should make a list of what is there already and whether you want to keep all of it. If you have a brand new plot, write down likes, dislikes, and the features that you would love to have. With existing gardens, make notes of the things that you want to get rid of and all the jobs that you have to learn how to do, such as pruning and feeding plants.

What have you got? The perimeter may be a hedge, a fence, or a wall, or a combination of all three. Some yards are what is termed open plan, with no demarcation screen at all, or only a curb to mark the boundary. Whatever it is, measure it and note the shape. Decide whether you are happy with it or if something different is needed for protection and privacy.

What size is your garden? Take measurements. Do the neighbors have any interesting features, or do you need to screen off an awful sight?

Is there a path? Do you want it, need it, like it? If there is no path, does that matter? How will you cross the yard in periods of prolonged wet weather? Make a note of areas of shade in the garden and discover what is causing the shadow. Is the garden in full sun, and at what time of day?

Think about the walls of the house, the boundary fence,

or the tool shed as areas that may be suitable for growing plants on – indeed, they may well benefit from a covering of climbing plants to disguise their appearance. There may be lots of existing trees and shrubs, or you could be the proud owner of a blank canvas with nothing but weeds.

Do you have a lawn? If so, is it big enough or even too big? Would you rather have more flowerbeds or a pond or a larger paved area for the barbecue and sun loungers?

Some plants are singularly unimpressive at certain times of the year and yet, when they decide to show off, the sight is unforgettable. Before making any decisions on the fate of existing plants, be patient and give them a year to show what they can do. Alternatively, call in an expert to label all the plants. Many excellent perennial plants and bulbs die down out of season, and you risk throwing them out with the weeds before you get to see them in their full glory.

What do you want? The first question that demands an answer is: Do you want to be a gardener? It may well be that you are only interested to the point that you have an area of ground and have to do something with it. Don't worry, you are in the majority, and it is a fact that many fanatical gardeners grew out of reluctant plot owners who felt that they had to "do" the gardening.

If you want a garden that leaves you time to put your feet up and relax with friends and children, then you should aim for a low-maintenance plot. There is no such thing as a no-maintenance garden, unless it has been entirely paved over, but there are ways to reduce the hours spent on boring repetitive tasks.

A good starting point is to decide how much time you can spend working in the garden each week. There will be busy times such as in late spring when everything starts to grow – including the weeds and the grass – and there will also be slack times in the dead of winter when you can stay out of the garden for longer periods.

For lots of average gardens and indeed gardeners, a Saturday morning's work is enough to keep it in good condition. Grass areas can run away with your allocated hours, especially if a quality, weed-free lawn is your aim. Do you want to grow your own vegetables and fruit? What about flowers? Lots of gardeners enjoy cutting flowers for the house, and a cutting bed of suitable plants means that other ornamental beds in the garden won't be denuded of color and interest.

How much can you afford to spend on the garden? I can't answer that for you, but even really small amounts of money can quickly make an enormous difference on the ground. Even gardeners can't get money to grow on trees, so it is a good idea to set a budget for each project, or your total allocation could disappear on one plan.

Do you have children or are you planning for old age? Or perhaps you are one of those people who sees your whole life in front of you and are thinking of both!

Most people now use their garden for entertainment, whether it be for childrens' parties or adults' barbecues or a glass of wine on the terrace, and suitable areas should be allowed for in the overall plan.

Check list

• Try to identify all the existing plants, with expert help if necessary. Be patient and don't dig up something and throw it away until you are sure that it looks dull for a substantial part of the year.
• Learn the difference between annual weeds that seed and die in the same year and perennial weeds that are difficult to get rid of, such as bindweed and couch grass.
• Keep an eye on the sun as it travels around your garden. Note which areas are in full sunshine, because they will be sunny and warm, while shaded areas will be colder.

Mixed planting of roses, stachys, begonias, and box leading to a vine-covered arbor. Notice how the curving beds create "secret" areas of lawn.

learning plant names

Do not be deterred by long, hard-to-pronounce names. Usually someone long before you has had the same problem and has come up with a common name such as sweet pea, mock orange, birch, or rose. Where the "proper" botanical name has an advantage is that everyone uses it, so you can converse with anyone, anywhere, and know you are talking about the same plant. Common names change within regions, never mind countries, and two plants may have the same common name. *Pulmonaria saccharata* and *Phlomis fruticosa* are unrelated, but both are sometimes called Jerusalem sage.

Botanical names are made up of at least two words, conventionally written in italics. The first word is for the genus, i. e., the group that the plant belongs to. Plants in the same genus share some characteristics, but may differ widely in others – trees and shrubs can belong to the same genus, but different species within the same genus may be evergreen or deciduous. The second word refers to the species, i. e., the kind of plant. Members of the same species are closely related – they will normally have the same height and spread, the same shape of leaf and flower, and can fertilize each other. Some plants then have a variety name, which is written without italics, enclosed in single quotation marks.

Quite often the species and variety names give you some description of the plant, so that *Rosa canina* is the dog rose and *Thymus vulgaris* is the common thyme, while the variety 'Aureus' is a common thyme with yellow leaves.

Most herbaceous plants have common as well as botanical names. *Verbascum* (the tall yellow spikes on the left) is also known as mullein; *Hemerocallis* (zones 3-10) (the orange flowers in the foreground) are day lilies.

Learning the language of plants

If all plants were just plants, a gardener's life would be rosy. But plants fall into categories, each with its own requirements. In time you will get to know the habits and needs of each type, but in the meantime you can grow the right plants by reading labels and finding out more information as you go along. There are dictionaries of plant terms containing lots of words you will never need – the following are the ones you are most likely to encounter.

Deciduous Plants that drop their leaves in winter, producing new foliage in the spring, such as oak or lilac.

Evergreen Plants that retain their leaves throughout the winter, including laurel, holly and conifers.

Hardy A plant that can survive outdoors all year round without protection. Obviously, plants that are hardy in a mild area may not be hardy in a colder area. North American gardeners are given guidance through a system of zones, of which zone 1 is the Arctic and zone 11 the southernmost part of the continent, where temperatures never reach freezing point. A plant may be hardy to, say, zones 7-9, which means you can leave it outdoors all winter if you live in Texas, but not if you live in New York.

Half-hardy Plants that need protection when the temperature drops to freezing.

Tender Plants that will suffer in cold weather, even before it reaches freezing point.

Acid loving Plants that grow best in soil that has a pH lower than 7 – i. e., soil that contains no lime. Such plants include rhododendrons and camellias, and are often also known as calcifuges (lime haters).

Alkaline (or lime) loving Plants that grow best in a soil that has a pH figure over 7 – i.e., soil that contains lime. Plants include lilac, the butterfly bush (buddleia), and fuchsia.

Rootstock The root and lower part of a plant onto which another variety is grafted.

Union The joint where the different variety is grafted on to the rootstock, usually causing a thickening of the stem.

Single, double, and semidouble Single flowers have a single whorl of petals. Most wild plants have single flowers. Semidouble flowers have two or three rows of petals in layers. Double flowers have many rows of petals and usually no stamens.

Annual A plant that germinates from seed, grows, flowers, and dies all in the same season; for example, snapdragons, marigolds, and sunflowers.

Biennial A plant that is sown in summer, overwinters outdoors, flowers in the following spring or early summer, and then dies; for example, foxgloves, sweet Williams, and Canterbury bells.

Herbaceous perennial Usually a plant that dies down in fall or winter, reappearing in the spring and flowering in the second year. Perennials live for at least two years, some for much longer, and include the familiar chrysanthemums and peonies.

Shrub A plant such as hydrangea which produces many woody stems from the base rather than a single trunk, like a tree. A **subshrub** is a shrub that is woody only at the base of the plant, such as perovskia, or one that dies back to ground level in winter, such as fuchsia.

Tree Usually thought of as a large plant with a single stem breaking into a crown of branches, such as a chestnut. But there are trees of all sizes, including some that never become big, such as the dwarf Japanese maples that provide wonderful fall color.

Conifer Usually an evergreen cone-bearing tree, such as a pine, but there are deciduous conifers, such as larch. Dwarf conifers are ideal for rockeries and small containers.

Bedding A general term for all those plants that provide seasonal color in flowerbeds, especially in summer, and are then removed and disposed of in the fall.

Climbers These plants clamber up and over walls, fences, and other plants. There are three groups: those that are self-clinging, using sucker pads, such as ivy; those that naturally twine around other plants (a good example is honeysuckle); and those that hold on using tendrils – sweet peas, for example.

Bulbs, corms, and tubers These are usually all called bulbs, but there is a difference. True bulbs, such as daffodils or onions, are made up of thickened leaves. Corms, by contrast, are thickened stems and are solid and hard. They include crocus and gladiolus. A tuber is a thickened root – a dahlia or a potato, for example – while a rhizome is a thickened underground stem, as seen in a bearded iris.

This deciduous azalea, variety 'Apple Blossom' (zones 5-8), requires an acid soil in light shade. If you provide the conditions your plants prefer – or choose plants to suit the conditions you are able to offer – they will reward you with health and beauty.

basic plant care

Get to know your soil — it's all that is keeping your plant alive. Is it light, dry, heavy, wet, or even waterlogged? Some plants are fussy, and they will be happy only if the soil is suitable for their needs.

Feeding the soil with the right nutrients can do a lot for a plant by encouraging growth, improving flower color, and increasing yields.

The right soil plus correct feeding equals happy plants.

Stone slabs make a handsome path down to a woodland garden. The beds around the shrubs and perennials are mulched with cedar bark.

down to earth

Plants in the garden will do better if they don't have to look after themselves and are given a little tender loving care. Spend five minutes each day looking around your garden to see that all the plants are enjoying your hospitality. The exercise will do you no harm, and you will get to know your plants.

cultivation

The point of cultivation is to break up the ground and make it more plant friendly, to allow plant roots to penetrate more readily in search of water and nutrients. If the area of ground to be cultivated is not too large, I recommend that you dig it by hand using a spade or garden fork, rather than cultivating it mechanically. Hand digging allows you to spot weed roots and pick them out and dump them. A rotavator just chops them up and leaves each piece to grow into a new weed. Soils that are in suitable condition for cultivating and not too wet are best dug in the late fall or early winter, turning the soil over and leaving it rough on the surface. Winter frost will break up the lumps, leaving the soil friable, and at the same time the chill will penetrate the soil, killing overwintering pests. Additives such as compost and grit can be applied at this stage, turning them into the soil as it is being dug.

Rotavating is a quick way to cultivate large areas, as the blades break the soil up, leveling it as they go. Heavy soils and those that haven't been worked for a season or more will require a rotavator that has a separate drive on the blades, allowing the wheels to turn independently. The wheels move slowly over the ground while the blades are revolving at speed to break up the soil. Try to cultivate during a dry spell; otherwise, the open ground soaks up the rain, becoming sodden and muddy. Trying to cultivate wet, muddy soil will destroy the soil structure and cause compaction, especially when you walk on it, resulting in poor drainage and sour soil that actually smells. By all means remove large stones and debris,

Geraniums, lady's mantle (*Alchemilla*), and forget-me-nots (*Myosotis*) growing wild in a neglected garden and as troublesome as any weed.

but don't try to cart away every last small stone since they keep the soil open and help drainage.

Knowing a weed when you see one Identifying weeds can be tricky. Some plants act like weeds, look like weeds, and even grow like weeds, but are in fact highly respectable plants. I always think of weeds as undesirable plants that in different circumstances would be planted in the garden. Some weeds are wild flowers. No one would suggest that Monet painted a field of weeds — of course not, it was a landscape of wild poppies. Some weeds disguise themselves with pretty flowers, such as bindweed with its pure white trumpets on twining, climbing stems. Then there is the dandelion, again with an attractive bloom, and what about the buttercup and thistle? Some of the worst weeds have an impressive pedigree — horsetail is hard to get rid of and that is hardly surprising, as it has been around since before the dinosaurs. Another really obnoxious plant is the bishop's weed, also called ground elder or gout weed, which doubles as a medicinal herb claimed to control gout and other ailments. But it also has an attractive variegated form I like to use for ground cover.

The whole identification problem is made worse by birds — they eat berries that pass through their digestive system unharmed and then germinate in your garden. In this way, shrubs such as cotoneaster, leycesteria, pyracantha, and daphne suddenly appear. If you don't recognize them in the seedling stage, they end up being composted – which is a pity, especially if you are in need of plants to fill any gaps in your beds. The best advice I can give is, if in doubt, leave unknown seedlings until the young plants are large enough to be identified as friend or foe. The illustrations on page 32 and 33 will help you identify the most common – and the worst – weeds. Some weeds are useful and even desirable in certain parts of the garden: stinging nettles encourage butterflies, and yellow rattleweed will help to weaken grass in a wild area by acting as a parasite and allowing the wild flowers to grow away in the weakened grass.

How weeds spread
Weeds can spread very quickly by seed, roots, and runners. It is very important that they are killed, dug up, or pulled out before they flower and produce seed, which germinates and in turn produces many more young weed plants. Bindweed spreads by white roots that are easily seen in the soil and should be dug out using a fork to reduce the risk of cutting the root. Even a small fragment will regrow. Try to remove as much as possible; it spreads rapidly. Weeds with a deep, fleshy root such as dock should be eased out of the ground without breaking the root, because any piece that remains in the soil will reroot. Creeping buttercup spreads rapidly by surface runners and left alone will soon cover a large area, killing lawn grass or weaker plants that you probably want to keep.

Methods of elimination
Once you have decided to eliminate the weeds, there are various well-tried and tested methods for attempting to remove them. The surest but most labor-intensive way is to dig them out and dump them. Deep digging, using a garden fork to remove all of the root is essential, as each piece of perennial weed root that is left will result in another plant.

• **Hoeing weeds** can be done in two ways, using different types of tool. A draw hoe or swan-neck hoe has a blade that is bent toward you and is used to chop or draw the weeds out of the ground; a push hoe is used to cut the weeds off below ground level or lift small weeds out. When the sun is shining, the hoed-off weeds can be left to wither and die, but if rain is expected, rake the weeds off or they will reroot into the damp soil. In rainy weather and when the ground is wet, stay off the beds and leave the weeding for a better day, as you will only destroy the surface of the soil.

• **Flame throwers**, which are handheld and powered by gas, are also effective – the flame is applied to the leaves of the weeds, burning them off. It works better on soft weeds and seedlings; larger weeds and those with a tough root system will regrow after a time.

• **Spraying with a chemical weedkiller** can be very successful, but read the instructions first and wear proper protective clothing. Chemicals such as glyphosate, which travels through the leaf into the stems and down into the root, killing the whole plant, are the most reliable. There are also contact weedkillers that work in the same way as the flame thrower, burning the foliage. Total weedkillers, which kill everything including the toughest plants, are available, but many of them contain chemicals that leave a residue in the soil, preventing anything from growing for up to 12 months.

• **Covering the soil with old carpet, black plastic, or landscape fabric** – a permeable membrane with a close weave to allow water and air through but no weeds to grow – can also kill weeds. Even the toughest perennial weeds can't survive if deprived of light for a long period. Mulch, providing it is at least 2 in (5 cm) deep, will help suppress the less vigorous weeds if it is spread on the soil surface. Old mushroom compost, wood chippings, bark mulch, and even old rotted farmyard manure will act as a mulch (see page 46 for more information).

Composting weeds
Be very careful which weeds you put on the compost pile. Those that spread by seeds should not be added, as the seeds will remain viable in the compost, growing away quite happily a year later when the compost is worked into the ground. Weeds such as thistle, dock, and bindweed that spread by root should have their roots removed and dumped before the stems and leaves are composted.

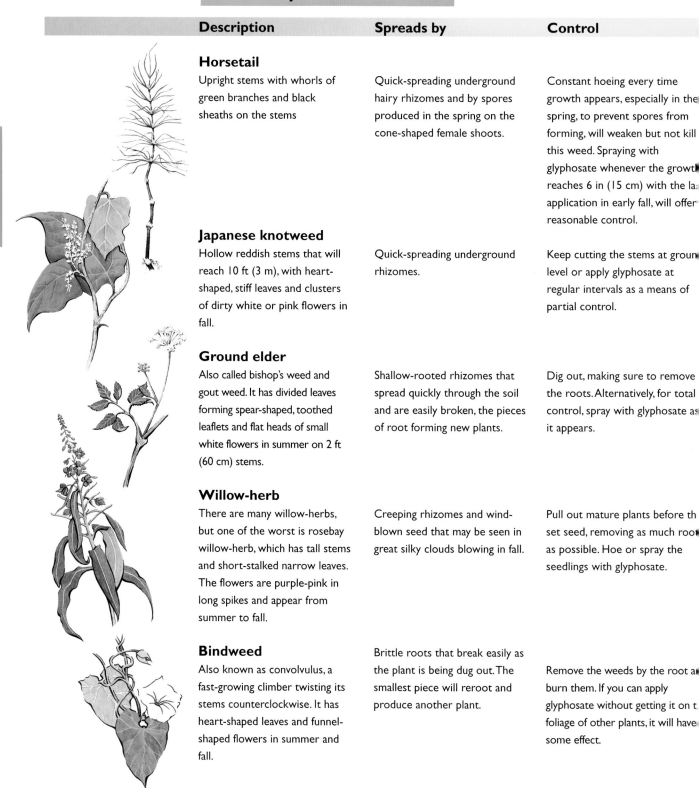

10 worst perennial weeds

Description	Spreads by	Control

Horsetail

Upright stems with whorls of green branches and black sheaths on the stems

Quick-spreading underground hairy rhizomes and by spores produced in the spring on the cone-shaped female shoots.

Constant hoeing every time growth appears, especially in the spring, to prevent spores from forming, will weaken but not kill this weed. Spraying with glyphosate whenever the growth reaches 6 in (15 cm) with the last application in early fall, will offer reasonable control.

Japanese knotweed

Hollow reddish stems that will reach 10 ft (3 m), with heart-shaped, stiff leaves and clusters of dirty white or pink flowers in fall.

Quick-spreading underground rhizomes.

Keep cutting the stems at ground level or apply glyphosate at regular intervals as a means of partial control.

Ground elder

Also called bishop's weed and gout weed. It has divided leaves forming spear-shaped, toothed leaflets and flat heads of small white flowers in summer on 2 ft (60 cm) stems.

Shallow-rooted rhizomes that spread quickly through the soil and are easily broken, the pieces of root forming new plants.

Dig out, making sure to remove the roots. Alternatively, for total control, spray with glyphosate as it appears.

Willow-herb

There are many willow-herbs, but one of the worst is rosebay willow-herb, which has tall stems and short-stalked narrow leaves. The flowers are purple-pink in long spikes and appear from summer to fall.

Creeping rhizomes and wind-blown seed that may be seen in great silky clouds blowing in fall.

Pull out mature plants before they set seed, removing as much root as possible. Hoe or spray the seedlings with glyphosate.

Bindweed

Also known as convolvulus, a fast-growing climber twisting its stems counterclockwise. It has heart-shaped leaves and funnel-shaped flowers in summer and fall.

Brittle roots that break easily as the plant is being dug out. The smallest piece will reroot and produce another plant.

Remove the weeds by the root and burn them. If you can apply glyphosate without getting it on the foliage of other plants, it will have some effect.

	Description	Spreads by	Control

Dock
Plants have a thick, carrotlike tap-root; tall, branched stem with large blunt leaves; and spikes of tiny red-green flowers from summer to fall.

Seed or pieces of root.

Dig out, taking care to remove all the root. Spray with glyphosate when the young, strongly growing foliage is present.

Quack grass
Other common names are couch, scutch, and twitch. A broad-leaved grass with spreading roots.

Rhizomes, which spread quickly to form a mat with growth buds all along the stem. The smallest piece of root will regrow.

Dig out, removing all the roots. Close cutting or spraying with glyphosate as the foliage appears will keep couch under control and, in time, will kill it.

Nettle
Tall straight stems with heart-shaped toothed leaves, often covered with stinging hairs. Greenish flowers hang in tassle-like clusters from summer to fall. Yellow roots.

Root and seed. Another quick spreader.

Easily hoed out at the seedling stage or dug out as large clumps – make sure you remove all the roots. Spray with glyphosate when growing strongly.

Buttercup
Deeply divided leaves and shiny deep yellow flowers in late spring and early summer.

Vigorous rooting runners, each producing many plants. Also spreads from seed.

Hand weeding or glyphosate if there are no other plants close by. A selective broad-leaved weedkiller may be used to kill unwanted buttercups in a lawn.

Dandelion
A rosette of long, toothed leaves and yellow daisylike flower. Flowers most of the year, peaking in late spring. The flowers are followed by circular heads of seeds, each with a parachute of feathery hairs.

Pieces of the fleshy taproot, or seed blown on the wind.

Dig the plant out before it sets seed, taking care to remove all the root. Spray with a broad-leaved weedkiller or use glyphosate, which should kill it in one application.

A raised mixed bed overlooking the sea, with pink, low-growing pelargoniums and salt-tolerant shrubs. Sitting on the wall brings you close to the plants.

making beds

I don't know how they became known as beds, but it is a name that covers all plantings, be they of flowers, fruit, vegetables, or shrubs. They can be any shape or size you like and surrounded by paths or grass.

Don't be too ambitious to start with. It is better to make a small bed and then enlarge it, than to go in at the deep end and decide later to make the area smaller. Decide on the general location of the bed and use the garden hose to mark the outline. Look at it from all parts of the yard to see that it is a pleasant shape and then view it from the house. If you have a two-story house, look at it from upstairs as well as down, because it will take on a completely different form when seen from above. Check that the proportions are right compared to everything else, and if the bed has a curved outline, make sure the bends are not too severe, since they could be difficult to cut with a mower.

Carving a bed from grass If you are making a bed from a lawn, the grass will need either to be killed by chemical weed control or to be removed by digging it into the ground, making sure the grass is buried in the bottom of the bed. Where there is a good depth of topsoil – at least 8 in (20 cm) – the grass sod can be skimmed off the surface with a spade and stacked out of the way, grass side down. It will rot down to form a humus-rich pile of soil. Start from within the proposed bed to avoid damaging the surface of the remaining lawn, and when wheeling debris away, don't use the same route over the grass each time or you will damage it. Edge the bed by leaving the soil surface 2 in (5 cm) below the grass – provided the edge isn't broken or flattened by feet, it will be acceptable. Stones, bricks on edge, and tiles can be used to form an edge, but where used to separate the lawn from the bed, they should be flush with the lawn surface; otherwise, the grass along the outer side of the perimeter will be difficult to cut.

Where there is no grass, the ground can be dug over and the stones and debris removed. Alternatively, stones can be recycled to form a firm base for a path or patio. Remove weed roots as you dig, and make sure the spade or fork goes in to the full depth of the blade or prongs, turning the soil over. Break up large, heavy lumps of soil with the spade, and when the soil dries out, rake it over to provide a fine tilth on the surface ready to receive seeds or plants.

Raised beds There are many advantages to forming raised beds in which the soil is artificially lifted above the surrounding ground. A 36 in (90 cm) wide bed may be raised by simply pushing up the soil to each side to form a mound, which provides better drainage for vegetables or more air circulation, for example, to reduce the risk of fungal diseases in strawberry plants. The effect is like the furrows and ridges in a plowed field.

If you want a contained bed, surrounding walls may be formed of brick or lumber, including railroad ties, and the bed filled in with layers of compost, farmyard manure, leaf mold, and topsoil. This not only avoids poor soil drainage, but allows you to grow plants even when the garden soil is unsuitable. Importing acidic soil will allow you to grow acid-loving plants such as rhododendron in a garden that is naturally limy. Gardeners who have difficulty bending to weed and plant, or those who work from a wheelchair, will find that raised beds are the answer.

Another type of bed is the seed bed, which is located in a sheltered position, so soil warms up quickly to get the seeds off to a good start and is easily worked to form a fine surface for sowing seeds.

Fork over the base of the bed for drainage. Form sides of boards or bricks.

Add layers of compost and farmyard manure and cover with topsoil.

Grow plants suited to the soil in the bed.

roots will have to compete for water and nutrients, resulting in a loss of vigor.

The correct spacing for plants can be tricky to achieve. The majority of plant labels give this information: if they don't, ask a knowledgeable sales assistant before purchasing. Remember that if the ultimate spread of the plant is 6 ft (2 m), that is 3 ft (1 m) on each side of the plant. If the plant beside it has the same spread, there should be at least 6 ft (2 m) space between the two plants. You can fill the gaps between the permanent plantings using short-lived plants such as annuals, bulbs, and biennials. These can be sacrificed as the main plants grow into the space, or in the case of longer-lasting perennials, they can be transplanted to fill other short-term gaps.

Transplanting Digging up a plant and replanting it in a

Herbs can be close planted, then thinned out as they mature.

different position is sometimes necessary, and the secret is not to let the plant know that it has been moved. Deciduous plants are best transplanted when they are dormant and without foliage. The exceptions are small birches, which should be moved as the leaves are falling, or when the leaf buds are swelling in spring. Move evergreen plants in late fall or early spring when there is some heat in the ground; then they will quickly make new

roots. In every case, it is essential that the plant is well watered immediately to settle the soil around the roots.

Small plants are easily lifted with little risk, but larger ones need special treatment to make sure they aren't set back by damaged roots, lack of water, or drying winds,

Rules for transplanting

- Transplant deciduous plants when they are dormant (i.e., when they have lost their leaves).
- Transplant evergreens in spring or fall when soil is warm.
- Prepare the new planting hole before lifting the plant.
- Incorporate some compost and bonemeal into the soil being returned to the planting hole.
- Lift the plant when the soil is moist, with as large a ball of soil as necessary to cover the roots.
- Wrap large root balls in burlap or plastic sheeting before moving the plant, to help keep the soil around the roots.
- Retain as many roots as possible, especially the small fibrous roots that collect water and nutrients. If roots are broken, prune them back, making a clean cut to reduce the risk of fungal diseases entering the wound.
- Firm the soil around the roots, making sure there are no air pockets.
- Water, water, and water the soil. Damp the foliage over to stop the leaves from transpiring. Then the roots won't have to work so hard to replace lost water to prevent wilting.
- Support the plant with a stake to prevent it from rocking in the wind.

which remove the moisture from the foliage. Covering with a tent of plastic or horticultural fleece will reduce water loss through the leaves by raising humidity and protecting the plant from biting cold winds that dry the leaf surface.

There are some plants that don't transplant well – you are unlikely to succeed in shifting pittosporum, broom, elaeagnus, daphne, ceanothus, hawthorn, or beech. Lilac, eucalyptus, and pyracantha dislike being moved after they have been in the ground a year.

Leaving space between the new plants gives them room to expand.
1. Lupines will spread to about 18 x 18 in (45 x 45 cm) and will also self-seed freely.
2. *Stachys byzantina* makes excellent ground cover and spreads to about 3 x 3 ft (90 x 90 cm).
3. *Dianthus* will achieve a spread of about 3 x 2 ft (90 x 60 cm).

1.

2.

3.

staking, training, and tying

It is the roots that keep the plant upright in the soil and prevent it from blowing over in a strong wind. Until the plant has had time to send roots out in all directions, it is easily knocked over. The larger the plant, the more subject it is to wind; small plants usually need only to have the soil firmed around the root area. Large shrubs and trees, especially those that are evergreen with leaves to catch the winter wind, need to be supported with a wooden or bamboo stake to prevent them from moving until the roots have spread out. The period of support depends upon the size of the plant, the amount of exposure, and the speed of growth, but it won't be less than one year.

What size stake? It is a mistake to use tall stakes that hold a tree so firmly that it doesn't make the effort to send its roots far and wide. A short stake that holds only the lower portion of the stem, allowing the top to sway, will support the roots and encourage the tree to thicken its stem so it is able to withstand wind. Wooden stakes should be treated with preservative to extend their lives. Round stakes with a point are easier to drive into the ground than pointed square stakes, which twist if they hit large stones.

Drive the stake into the prepared hole before planting, to avoid damaging the roots. Place the plant in front of the stake to screen it and spread the roots out in the hole, allowing them to go in every direction.

The soil should be returned to the planting hole, filling it in around the roots so there are no large air pockets and firming it in as you go. Leave the surface slightly "dished" to retain water long enough for it to soak in around the roots. Continue to water the root area as often as necessary to stop the soil from drying out.

Using tree ties The plant should be firmly secured to the stake using a proper tie and pad. This is placed around the main stem of the plant and fastened to the support

1. Drive the stake into the hole and the solid soil before inserting the tree, to avoid damaging the roots.

2. Position the stem close to, but not touching, the stake. Train the roots around the stake.

3. & 4. Support the tree with a tie and pad, making sure to nail the pad to the stake and not the trunk.

with a buckle. If it is a large stake, the tie can be nailed to the stake. A rubber buffer or pad can be placed between the stake and the stem to prevent rubbing. Bulky shrubs with more than one stem can be held in place with an old pair of tights, the legs woven through the branches and tied to the stake. The ties need to be checked in spring and again in fall to make sure they are not cutting into the bark, causing damage, and restricting the stem.

Other means of support

• Climbing plants including rambling and climbing roses also require support and something to cling to and scramble over. Trellis or wooden laths can be put on walls with masonry nails with a 2 in (5 cm) wooden spacer to leave a gap between the wall and the support to allow space for the plant shoots to twine themselves around the wood. Where stems are being tied to a support, you should use soft garden twine or raffia to prevent damage to the shoot. Keep the loop loose enough to allow the stem to thicken up without being constricted.

• Galvanized training wire, which won't rust, can be strung on the wall and spaced horizontally 12 in (30 cm) apart to train shoots of wisteria along or to tie in the branches of fruit trees to form a framework. Trained trees of apple, pear, and peach – often called espaliers – on a sunny wall will reward you with good crops. Masonry nails with strips of soft lead attached (sold as lead-headed nails) are good for training stems into position, using the lead to hold the stem. As the branches thicken, the lead strips unbend without damaging the bark.

• Netting wire or plastic mesh can be used to support vigorous climbers such as honeysuckle, clematis, and jasmine, and tall varieties of sweet pea, which will use their tendrils to twine around and provide a good grip.

• Peas and beans are best supported on pea sticks. These are twiggy hedge prunings about 36 in (90 cm) long inserted into the seed bed along the rows of peas. They support the plants as they climb, keeping the pods off the ground and making picking easy.

Apple variety 'Orléans Reinette' against a warm, sunny wall. This shape, known as an espalier, is achieved by training the branches across wire or stakes so they grow horizontally.

• Some herbaceous perennials need to be supported, especially tall plants such as campanula, verbascum, and delphinium. There are lots of patented frames and wire supports on the market, but a word of caution: when thin stakes like bamboo are being used, cover the tops with corks or small plastic pots to prevent eye damage when bending over to work in the bed.

Arches and arbors There are many other forms of framework used to support plants. Metal and wooden arches at entrances and over paths look charming, but before ordering or purchasing check that, when they are covered with climbers, there will still be space to walk through. Obelisks covered with scented sweet peas will fit into the smallest garden, and a wooden arbor draped in vines, complete with grapes, and shading a patio, are two other ways of supporting your plants.

Overleaf: an obelisk supports sweet peas in this scented garden.

mulching

A mulch is a layer of material on the soil surface, usually around plants, that reduces garden maintenance and is of benefit to the plants. Mulching helps to suppress weeds, improves soil structure, encourages plants to make good growth, and enhances the appearance of the bed.

• If a mulch is applied to moist soil, it will help to prevent evaporation and keep the soil cool in summer.
• In winter a deep mulch will act like a blanket, keeping the soil warmer and preventing it from freezing, so that planting can take place.
• While no mulch on its own is effective against strongly growing perennial weeds, it will stop weeds from germinating in the soil underneath, and any weeds that do grow in the loose mulch are easily removed.
• As organic mulches such as farmyard manure rot down, they add humus and some nutrients to the soil.

Types of mulch   There are three types of mulch: organic or humus mulches; inorganic mulches such as gravel; and suppressants such as carpet and landscape fabric.

Organic mulches include rotted farmyard manures, leaf mold, garden compost, spent mushroom compost, bark mulch, and grass clippings. If these mulches are applied in a layer at least 2 in (5 cm) thick, they will do a good job. As they decompose, they use up nitrogen-fixing bacteria, and it is worthwhile increasing the rate of nitrogen fertilizer to compensate. Bark mulch, if used fresh, can contain diseases and is best if decomposed before applying. Grass clippings should only be used as a light mulch; a thick layer will turn into a slimy mess.

There is a selection of hard materials that can be used for mulching. Gravels are available in a range of colors and grades; horticultural grit is a coarse grade of sand; pea gravel is larger; then there are round smooth river stones up to 6 in (15 cm) in size. Gravel warms up quickly, giving off its heat. The paler gravels reflect the light and make a good surface mulch for hot beds for sun-loving plants.

Weed suppressants include old carpet, plastic, woven polypropylene, and newspaper. None of them is attractive, but if they are left in place for a year, the weeds will be killed through lack of light. With the exception of plastic sheeting, they all allow water to penetrate to the soil below. Add a topping of bark, and no one will know they are there; yet you will have effective weed control.

When to mulch   A mulch acts as a blanket, preserving the soil in the same condition as when it is applied. If the soil is cold and wet, it will remain that way, and the same goes for hot and dry conditions. The best time to mulch is when the soil is moist and warm, providing ideal conditions for growth – spring is the traditional season for mulching.

How to mulch   If there are annual weeds growing on the bed, hoe them off or spray with glyphosate weedkiller. If you use weedkiller, don't apply the mulch for 10 days or until the weeds turn yellow. Rake the soil over to remove stones and debris, and give a feed of a balanced fertilizer at 1 oz per sq yd (30 g per sq m). Spread the mulch evenly all over the bed, at least 2 in (5 cm) deep, keeping it away from the stems of the plants, because it could cause soft stems to rot. Where supplies are scarce or expensive, apply the mulch as no more than a collar around each plant, covering the root zone. Weeds will grow where there is no covering, but the plants will still get the benefit of the mulch.

Depending what type of organic mulch has been used, top it up as it rots down. This is usually done each spring, applying the new layer directly on top of the old mulch.

A deep mulch helps to retain moisture in the soil and will reduce the need to weed. *Bergenia* (1), the New Zealand flax *Phormium tenax* (2), *Gunnera manicata* (3), and moisture-loving ferns (4) will all benefit from this treatment.

pruning

There is no great mystery to pruning. Common sense is the main requisite, followed by clean, sharp tools. To prune is simply to cut off branches that are not wanted. This can be for a variety of reasons such as overcrowding, branches crossing each other and rubbing, or diseased stems – for example, canker on apple branches. Some plants produce their flowers or fruit on new growths and are cut to encourage more young shoots. There are plants that need to be cut hard each year, removing most of the growth made during the previous year; they include buddleia (butterfly bush), ribes (flowering currant), and syringa (lilac). Equally, there are some plants that require little or no regular pruning, and they include shrubs such as daphne, hebe, and pieris.

Pruning for shape – topiary (see page 51) – is on the increase, and evergreen plants clipped into the shape of objects and animals are fun to do. Fruit trees are trained and pruned for maximum crop against a wall, and fan, cordon, and espalier shapes are all popular.

Pruning is also necessary to remove unwanted material, such as suckers of the parent plant growing from below the graft and weakening the plant. Evergreen variegated plants sometimes produce a rogue shoot that is the original green without any variegation. If this is not removed, it will grow more quickly, taking over the plant and eventually smothering out the variegation.

Pruning the branches out of the center of a thorny gooseberry plant makes life a lot easier when it comes to picking the crop.

Diseased branches need to be cut out well below the diseased part and burned, as in the case of rose black spot and apple canker.

Pruning tools A knife, pair of clippers, small hand saw, shears, and a pair of loppers are sufficient for most jobs, and I would strongly recommend that you buy the best you can afford. They will need to be kept sharp; good steel takes and keeps a good edge, and that sort of quality costs money.

Pruning shrubs Before tackling any shrub, find out when it flowers. Deciduous shrubs fall into three categories for pruning.

• Winter-flowering deciduous shrubs need very little pruning apart from the removal of diseased branches and those that are growing toward the center. Young plants will need to be shaped, removing any stems that are causing the plant to be lopsided. The time to prune is immediately after the flowers have faded.

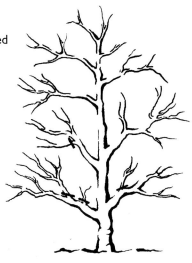

Winter-flowering shrubs: prune only to maintain shape or to remove dead or diseased wood.

• Spring- and early summer-flowering deciduous shrubs are pruned as soon as flowering is finished. First remove any diseased or thin shoots, then cut all the branches that flowered to within a few buds of the base and leave the new shoots to flower next year.

Spring and early summer-flowering shrubs: prune immediately after flowering. By mid- to late fall, the young shoots will have grown vigorously and produced new shoots on which next year's flowers are borne.

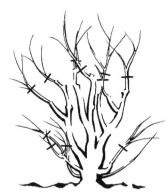

Late summer-flowering shrubs should be pruned in early spring. In the first year, cut out only damaged or weak shoots.

In the second year, cut back the last season's growth by half, cutting just above strong outward-pointing buds.

In subsequent years, cut back to within one or two buds of the previous year's growth.

• Late summer-flowering shrubs are pruned in late spring when any risk of frost has passed. Again, remove diseased and thin shoots, and prune out last year's flowering shoots, allowing the new growths to grow away and flower later in the year.

Deciduous shrubs that have been neglected and are overgrown can be pruned hard, removing the old shoots to the base to encourage new growth. If all the branches are cut, there will be no flowers that year, and an alternative is to cut down half each year, leaving the other half to flower.

There are some deciduous shrubs that are grown for their colored stems such as *Cornus alba*, and the best color is produced on young shoots. The plant should be cut to ground level each spring and allowed to grow strongly all summer, coloring up in early winter.

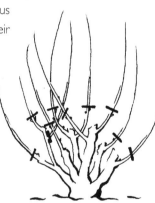

To promote colorful stems, cut back hard in early spring.

Pruning evergreen shrubs
To avoid any risk of frost damage to tender new shoots, prune evergreens in early summer. Remove diseased, thin, and spindly shoots, and if the plant needs to be thinned out, remove branches from various parts to prevent it from becoming one-sided. Evergreens with large leaves such as laurel should be cut with clippers rather than shears to avoid making the plant look messy with leaves cut in half.

Pruning trees You can prune young trees so they have a good shape and the main branches are well apart, to make a balanced tree later in its life. Branches that are low to the ground and those crossing into the center of the tree can be removed. Where a tree forks and the angle where the branches join is very narrow, remove one of the branches to reduce the risk of their splitting in a storm. When you are removing a large heavy branch, do it in stages to reduce the weight and prevent the limb from tearing off and damaging the main trunk. Always make a saw cut partway in, on the underside of the branch, before cutting from the top. This stops the bark from tearing off beyond the cut.

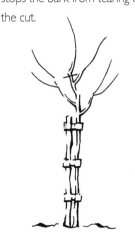

Prune young trees in mid-fall, cutting each branching stem to within 12–18 in (30–45 cm) of the main stem.

Once the tree is about five years old, prune only to maintain the desired shape.

Fun with topiary: a woman gardener (left) in box, with box hedging containing the herbs; a crocodile (above) formed from *Lonicera nitida* (zones 6-9) in a spring garden.

Pruning Hedges

Pruning promotes growth, which can be used to your advantage with hedges. When you cut a shoot, it will send out two or three new shoots and the plant becomes thicker and more dense. By regularly clipping a hedge, it thickens out with no gaps. Old hedges that are bare at the base can be cut hard, encouraging new shoots from the base. These, themselves, can then be clipped to thicken them up and cover the bareness.

Topiary

Topiary is the art of shaping plants into objects. It is a form of hedge cutting and can be practiced on a great variety of plants. Choose a simple shape to start with: I would hate for you to cut the head off the peacock just as you have got the tail exactly right. Ball or cone shapes are fairly easy to do, and a matched pair can look good at the top of steps or on each side of an entrance. Trim the shoots evenly and regularly with clippers, making sure the plant doesn't lack water or nutrients. More complicated objects are best grown within a wire outline of the desired shape and clipped to build up the bulk. The final shaping is refined as the growths reach the wire outline. Even a moderate fall of snow can play havoc with topiary. The weight bends the branches, opening the plant and spoiling the shape, so brush it off as soon as it falls.

Plants suitable for topiary

Buxus sempervirens (box) (zones 6-8)
Ligustrum ovalifolium (privet) (zones 8-9)
Lonicera nitida (shrubby honeysuckle) (zones 6-9)
Taxus baccata (yew) (zones 7-8)
Thuja occidentalis (arbor vitae) (zones 2-7)

Pruning other plants

There is no reason to worry about pruning either roses or clematis. Some experts make it sound difficult and complicated, but that is only because there are so many different types of each. Once you know the type of rose – for example, a climber or a shrub rose – the pruning is no more difficult than for any other plant. The pruning of each is covered under clematis and roses on pages 160 and 163 respectively.

propagation

Seeds or plants There are advantages and disadvantages in growing from seed rather than buying plants, and you would be a poor gardener if you did not use both methods to fill the garden. With seed sowing there is the satisfaction of producing your own plants from start to finish, and in the case of annuals, the time from sowing to flowering can be as little as eight weeks. Then there is the cost factor, where a pack of seed is a fraction of the price of one plant and will result in lots of plants. The cost disappears altogether if you collect seed from your own plants that will reproduce similar to the parent: species delphiniums (rather than cultivars) will do this, as will some marigolds (calendula)

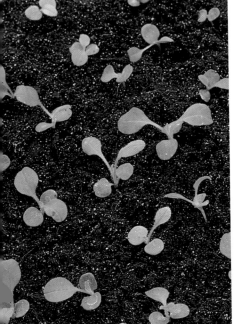

Seedlings pricked out and spaced in soil. The healthiest specimens have been selected and given plenty of room to grow.

and money plant (lunaria), for example. On the other hand, if you save your own seed of a named variety of sweet pea that is all the same color and sow it, you will produce sweet pea plants in a whole range of colors.

There is a bigger range of varieties available in seeds than of plants that are carried by most garden centers. But buying plants is also rewarding in that you immediately have a plant that may already be in flower, and you will have avoided any possible problems of germination and growing on and caring for the young plant until it is ready to plant out.

Some plants are not worth growing from seed, for example, hebe, a shrub that is easy to grow quickly from a cutting. Others such as rhododendron take years to produce flowers when grown from seed, and after all that time may not be the same as the parent – your original seedling may turn out to be a useless plant with poor flower color and a bad growth habit.

Growing from seed There are two methods of seed sowing that interest the "down-to-earth" gardener: sowing outside directly into the soil and sowing seeds in a glasshouse or on a windowsill in flats or pots of seed medium.

Direct sowing in the garden soil A perfectly acceptable way of growing plants – after all, it's nature's way. The seeds can be sown in rows and then transplanted to their permanent positions when they are big enough to handle. Or they can be "broadcast," sown by scattering the seed into the soil where they are to flower: this method is often used for displays of annual flowers for summer color.

Biennials such as wallflowers and perennials such as hollyhocks are often sown in early summer in rows outdoors and the seedlings transplanted to their permanent positions in the fall.

Seed is available in a range of options to suit your needs.
- The most popular is still loose seed in a sealed pack.
- If you find fine seed flows between your fingers too quickly, resulting in a forest of seedlings all jammed together, try pelleted seed where each seed is coated to form a little pellet not unlike a sweet pea seed and just as easy to handle.
- Another foolproof method is a line of seeds prespaced in a strip of "tape" that dissolves when the seeds are in the ground and watered.

Tips for successful sowing outside

- Buy hardy varieties of seed that are recommended for growing outdoors

- Before opening the seed pack, make a label written with a waterproof pen on a plastic strip, stating the variety and the date of sowing and insert it at the end of the row before you sow.

- Check the pack as to the depth to sow the seed: it can vary from surface sowing with a mere dusting of horticultural sand to cover the seed, to 2 in (5 cm) deep in the case of some beans.

- If the pack states that spring is the time to sow seed outdoors, don't read that literally as the first day of the spring. What it means is when the soil has warmed up and is moist but not wet and any risk of frost has passed. Then is the time to cultivate the soil and rake the surface to remove any stones.

- The surface of the soil must be firm, dry, and fine with no lumps. Remember, the tiny shoot that emerges from the seed has to get to the surface and the daylight as quickly as possible. A lump of soil or a stone will prevent that from happening, and the seedling will die.

- When sowing in rows, use a length of string and two short sticks – a gardener's "line" – to mark the row. Form the drill at the depth recommended by pulling the end of a rake or the corner of a hoe along the line. If the soil has been properly prepared, there will be no lumps or large stones in the drill.

- Sow the seed thinly to allow each seedling space to grow without competition.

- Once the seed has been sown in the drill, cover it to the correct depth with fine soil or horticultural sand if specified, and gently firm with your foot. Water the rows of seeds with a fine rose on the end of the watering can or hose.

- Some varieties of seed such as lettuce or marigolds (*Calendula*) will be germinated and showing after a week or ten days, while other types such as parsley or sweet Williams can take much longer – up to nine weeks – so resist the temptation to scrape the soil away to see what is happening.

- Have faith, most seeds manage to grow even if the conditions are not perfect.

- Transplant seedlings by easing them out of the soil using a hand fork and taking care not to damage the roots. Hold the seedling by the leaves and not by the stem, which is easily bruised, allowing fungus disease into the wound and killing the plant. Replant at the spacing recommended on the seed pack and at the same depth as the seedling was growing before. If you have plants to spare, you can thin out and throw away the surplus, leaving the rest in place at the correct spacing.

Young transplanted cabbage plants covered with netting to prevent birds – especially pigeons – from eating them. The fruit cage in the background also protects crops from hungry birds. This sort of protection is useful if you have a cat, or if your plants are likely to be attacked by rabbits, deer, or other wildlife.

Tips for successful sowing indoors

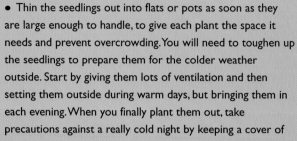

Seed sown in a glasshouse or on a windowsill in seed flats or even used yoghurt cups with drainage holes in the base, filled with a special seed medium, will germinate more quickly than outside in the cold. The seedlings must then be "hardened off" before they can be planted out. This is done by leaving the plants out during the day and bringing them in at night until they become acclimatized to the outside temperature.

• Sow the seed at the right time, depth, and temperature as recommended on the seed pack. The soil should be fine, with no coarse material and low in nitrogenous fertilizer, as you want sturdy plants rather than soft lush growth.

• Water the seed medium after sowing using a fine rose on the watering can. Thoroughly wet the soil rather than just dampening the surface.

• Cover the soil with newspaper to keep it warm and dark until the seeds germinate. Remove it before the seedlings become leggy from lack of light.

Pots and flats of seedlings on a glasshouse bench, all well labeled and growing away. Once the seedlings are sturdy enough to handle, they can be transplanted into larger containers and eventually moved outside.

• Thin the seedlings out into flats or pots as soon as they are large enough to handle, to give each plant the space it needs and prevent overcrowding. You will need to toughen up the seedlings to prepare them for the colder weather outside. Start by giving them lots of ventilation and then setting them outside during warm days, but bringing them in each evening. When you finally plant them out, take precautions against a really cold night by keeping a cover of horticultural fleece handy.

Any surplus seedlings can be grown on in pots or given to friends or, as a last resort, composted.

• Hold seedlings by the leaves, not by the stems, which bruise easily, allowing disease to enter. Damping off is a fungus disease that seedlings are prone to and can be caused by overcrowding, unsterilized soil, damp conditions, and damaged plants. Seedlings rot at the stem base, then keel over and die. Watering the seedlings with a solution of Cheshunt compound (a fungicide) will prevent damping off.

• Don't allow the soil to dry out since it is hard to wet again and it doesn't take much of a check in growth for the plants to die.

What terms mean

Hardening off Gradually getting plants acclimatized to lower temperatures so that they don't suddenly recieve a severe setback when they are planted out.

Thinning out Reducing the number of plants in a container or outside bed to allow the remaining seedlings space to develop.

Pricking out Transferring seedlings to space them out and give them room to grow.

Dibble To form a hole in the soil using a tool called a dibbler, to plant seedlings or sow large seeds.

Broadcast To sow seed at random, scattering it over the soil, for example, sowing grass seed for a lawn.

Drill A narrow V-shaped depression made in the soil to sow seed in, or the actual row of seedlings that has germinated.

Opposite: **A clean glasshouse with concrete floor, good ventilation, lots of light, and sturdy staging provides the ideal conditions for growing cacti from seed. They can be slow to germinate, but are worth the wait.**

dividing plants

This is one of the important methods of propagating and a way for the most inexperienced gardener to increase plants with as good as 100 percent success. The types of plants that lend themselves to division are those that form mats, tufts, or clumps, and include many perennials, alpines, water plants, and even some suckering shrubs such as kerria. Some plants dislike being disturbed; they include the peony and Christmas rose and those plants with thick main roots but few fibrous roots, such as the oriental poppy and lupine.

In addition to increasing the number of plants, dividing is a good way of rejuvenating an old clump, by retaining and planting the young rooted pieces from the outer edge and discarding the older woody center. Division is carried out in either the fall or in the spring. I prefer the spring when the plants are just starting to grow, the weather is improving, and they have the whole summer to produce a large plant before they die down for the winter.

How to divide a plant Dig up the clump when the foliage is starting to grow, taking care not to damage the roots. Remove any surplus soil. Clumps with fibrous roots that are not matted together may be teased apart, separating them into small pieces of plant complete with roots. You can prize apart dense clumps using garden forks or, in some cases, solid masses of hostas can be cut with a knife or a spade. Any plants that have become infested with perennial weeds should not be used: it is difficult to separate the roots, and if one piece of weed root is missed, it can grow away, protected by the plant.

Replant the new plants as quickly as possible to prevent their growth from being checked by a long spell out of the soil. Plant them in well-cultivated soil, free of weeds and dressed with some bonemeal. Water the plants in, to settle the soil around the roots.

Growing from cuttings Taking and rooting plants from cuttings is the most satisfactory gardening job of all. There is real pleasure when you ease a piece of plant out of the soil and see the mass of roots. It is particularly satisfying to be able to root plants that are listed as difficult. Years later, you will still remember the plant you rooted and where it came from before it ended up in your garden. There is a story behind every plant you manage to propagate this way.

There are lots of ways of rooting cuttings that will become plants identical to their parents. The easiest foolproof methods are from softwood cuttings in summer and from hardwood cuttings in winter.

Softwood cuttings Softwood means exactly that; you use the current year's shoots that are soft but not floppy. You cut them about 2-4 in (5-10 cm) long in late spring and early summer, before the stem becomes hard and woody, and root them in a container of medium, covering them with clear plastic to prevent wilting. When they are rooted, which can be in as short a time as six weeks, they can be repotted or planted out in the garden. This is a quick, cheap way to increase a whole range of shrubs, perennials, and alpines, especially if you have a good source of cuttings. Friends with gardens are usually only too pleased to offer pieces, and if you ask your local park manager, he might cut you a few suitable stems. The one thing that you must not do, of course, is to take cuttings without permission in anyone else's garden.

Honeysuckle (*Lonicera*) is easy to propagate from softwood cuttings in summer, as well as from hardwood cuttings in winter.

pests and diseases

You will soon find that pests and diseases are completely natural in the garden, and hopefully you will be able to live with them without declaring all-out war. There is a need to be constantly vigilant for a serious attack, but a few creepy crawlies or diseased spots are usually of no consequence. Mind you, I suppose that the Great Famine of Ireland, partly caused by blight on potatoes, started as a few spots on a leaf or two.

Diseases such as black spot defoliate the plant, while viruses distort the leaves and stunt the plant. Canker can kill even a mature tree by completely ringing the bark and preventing the flow of water and nutrients. Fruit trees are particularly vulnerable.

Blight isn't confined to potatoes – tomatoes may develop the same symptoms.

Good hygiene both outside and under cover in a glasshouse or plastic tunnel will go a long way toward preventing diseases. Removing decaying material will reduce the spread of botrytis or gray mold and some of the mildews, and a movement of air will reduce the high humidity that helps spread fungal spores.

Not all insects are pests; indeed, many garden visitors are on our side, helping to eliminate the troublemakers and keep a balance. Ladybugs and their larvae, plus the larvae of hoverflies and lacewings eat enormous quantities of aphids (greenfly). Spiders are to be welcomed in the garden as they eat all sorts of pest insects.

Frogs and toads help to keep the population of slugs and snails at acceptable levels, while many small birds eat

This aphid attack on a honeysuckle flower is both unsightly and potentially damaging to the plant's growth.

aphids. When chemicals are used to kill pests, they also destroy the natural predators that, over time, could multiply to a level where the chemicals would not be needed.

Sometimes you can't leave everything to nature. Some pests can cause enormous damage. Those that suck the sap of the plant, such as greenfly, whitefly, and blackfly, cause the leaves to become distorted; and they also spread diseases, including viruses. They exude a sticky honeydew, which becomes moldy, turning black and disfiguring the leaves.

Earwigs are a pest of the summer and fall when they damage the blooms of chrysanthemums and dahlias. Then there are the caterpillars of the cabbage white butterfly that munch their way through leaves at an alarming rate, but it is the pests in the ground that I dislike most. Vine weevils, leatherjackets, and chafer grubs all do enormous damage to the roots of plants, while alien flat worms eliminate the benefical earthworm.

Larger pests include moles (did you know that there are no moles in Ireland?), mice, rats, and other vermin, plus some birds that can cause annoyance in the garden by devouring transplanted green vegetable seedlings.

Earwig

Easily recognized by the pincers at the rear of the body, earwigs are shiny brown and over ½ in (15 mm) long.

Attacks The foliage and flowers of many plants, leaving a ragged hole. Chrysanthemums and dahlias are particularly prone to attack, and their flowers may be destroyed.

Prevention Earwigs like to hide in the dark during the day, and one way to trap them is to hang an upside-down flowerpot filled with straw on a stake among the plants. Shake the pot over a bag every afternoon to release the pests, then dump the bag.

Control Earwigs feed in the evening, and you can catch lots if you patrol with a flashlight. Insecticides are best applied in the early evening all over the plants, taking care that the chemical doesn't mark the flowers.

Gooseberry sawfly

There are three different gooseberry sawflies, but it is their caterpillars that do the damage. All three larvae grow to ¾ in (20 mm) long and are pale green; two of them are marked with black spots.

Attacks The foliage of the gooseberry plant just as the fruit is ripening, quickly stripping off the leaves to leave only the main vein and the leaf stalk. Red and white currants are also attacked.

Prevention None.

Control Inspect the plants daily from mid-spring, especially under the leaves where the eggs are laid. Remove the caterpillars by hand or spray with pyrethrum.

Carrot fly

It is the maggot (larva) of the carrot fly that causes the damage. The creamy yellow grub is almost ½ in (10 mm) long, and up to three generations may be born between late spring and fall.

Attacks Carrots are the main host, but celery, parsnip, and parsley are also subject to attack. The fly lays its eggs close to the plant, and the maggot tunnels into the root. Tunnels close to the surface show as brown lines on the root. Other rots enter the wounds, and the root becomes useless. Parsley foliage turns yellow, and the plant may die.

Prevention The fly is attracted by the smell of the foliage, so sow sparsely to avoid having to thin the seedlings, which is what causes the distinctive smell. The fly is low-flying, so if a barrier such as a horticultual fleece 12 in (30 cm) high is erected around the crop, the fly will be unable to get through to lay its eggs. Sow after the first generation of maggots has emerged in late spring, and crops harvested before late fall will miss the second generation.

Control Varieties of carrot that are less subject to damage include 'Flyaway' and 'Systan.' There are dusts available that can be applied to the seed drill at sowing time.

Aphids

Aphids are sometimes known as greenfly, although they may be brown, black, yellow, pink, or gray in color and are usually ½-⅛ in (2–3 mm) in length. As they grow, they cast their skins and may be mistaken for other insects.

Attacks There are few plants that aphids don't feed on, but they are common on beech, linden, and cherry trees, roses, honeysuckle, beans, and lettuce. They suck the sap, weakening the plant and causing stunted growth. As they feed, they exude a sticky honeydew on the lower leaves, which becomes moldy and black, resembling soot. Virus disease (see page 68) is spread by aphids.

Prevention There is no successful way to prevent aphids in the garden.

Control Insecticides, including systemic chemicals that are absorbed by the plant and kill the aphids when they suck the sap, are effective, but it is necessary to change the chemical regularly, as the aphids will, in time, build up immunity to most products. Organic treatments include pyrethrum and soaps. There are beneficial insects such as the hoverfly and the ladybug that devour aphids and help to keep them under control.

Caterpillars

These are the larval stage of moths and butterflies, and are usually long and thin with an obvious head, three pairs of legs at the front, and two to five pairs on their abdomen. They come in all colors and quantities of hair, depending on the type.

Attack Most of the well-known pest caterpillars, such as the larvae of the large and small cabbage white butterfly, feed on leaves. Others, including cutworms, feed on roots and codling moth larvae feed on fruit.

Prevention Pheromone traps may be used to trap the male codling moth, preventing mating and reducing the number of maggots attacking the apple crop. Picking off the caterpillars when

you see them is a help, and since some feed at night, a patrol in the evening with a flashlight will catch a lot. Planting nasturtiums close to cabbages will divert the butterflies, and as the young caterpillars appear on the leaves, they can be picked off, leaf and all, and dumped or flattened with a heavy heel.

Control Pyrethrum may be used as an organic spray. Alternatively, try the biological control *Bacillus thuringiensis*.

Leatherjacket

These gray-brown tubular larvae can grow up to 1½ in (4 cm), and are found in the soil. They are the larvae of the cranefly (daddy-long-legs), which lays its eggs in late summer, usually in long grass.

Attacks New lawns, causing serious damage by eating the grass roots and causing the plants to turn yellow. They will also eat the roots of vegetables, strawberries, and seedlings.

Prevention The easiest way to get rid of them in a lawn is to irrigate the grass and then cover it overnight with black plastic. The leatherjackets will come to the surface and can be cleared up in the morning or left for the birds' breakfast.

Control Insecticides such as lindane dust are effective only against the young larvae. If the soil is damp and above 58°F (14°C), nematodes (*Steinernema*) are effective against all larval stages.

Slugs and snails

These are similar enough to be lumped together, although snails have shells and so prefer a limy soil, which supplies the calcium to make their home. Slugs mainly live below ground. Both secrete a slimy mucus that dries to a silvery trail to show where they have been. Providing the temperature stays above 40°F (5°C), slugs will feed all winter.

Attack Leaves, flowers, and stems, destroying the foliage of many plants, notably hostas. They also attack tender spring shoots, seedlings, and fruit, including tomatoes.

Prevention It is not possible to eradicate slugs and snails from the garden, and the best form of prevention is to stop them from getting to the plants. A layer of coarse grit spread over the soil surface will deter them from crawling on their bare tummies. A strip of copper wire around the rim of pots and trays of seedlings is effective, as slugs and snails won't crawl over the copper. Good hygiene helps – removing debris and leaves will leave them with nowhere to hide during the day.

Control Slugs and snails are very active at night and can be picked off by flashlight. Poisoned pellets are effective in dry weather, but some are dangerous to dogs and cats and need to be used with care. Trap by placing small containers of beer at ground level – the slugs and snails fall in and drown. Try biological control using the nematode *Phasmarrhabditis* in spring and fall when the temperature is above 40°F (5°C), but it is not very effective against snails living above ground.

Whitefly

Glasshouse whitefly are sap-feeding insects $\frac{1}{12}$ in (2 mm) in size with white wings. When disturbed they will fly around. The nymphs are green-white and immobile, and are found on the underside of leaves.

Attacks Under glass, whitefly is a real pest of crops and houseplants. Both the fly and the nymph excrete a sticky honeydew onto the leaves which becomes moldy and turns black. Tomatoes and fuchsias are particularly prone to attack.

Prevention There is no real prevention.

Control The parasitic wasp *Encarsia formosa* is the best form of biological control, provided it is introduced into the glasshouse before large numbers of whitefly emerge. Insecticides other than soap will kill *Encarsia,* and whitefly quickly build up resistance to most insecticides anyway. As an alternative, hang sticky yellow traps early in the season to catch whitefly before they mutiply.

Red spider mite

There are three common types of spider mite – fruit, conifer, and glasshouse – but it is the latter that is the most troublesome. The mites are tiny – less than $\frac{1}{25}$ in (1 mm) with four pairs of legs – and, without a magnifying glass, they look like pepper on the back of the leaf. They color in the fall from pale green to orange-red, producing a fine web from leaf to leaf.

Attacks Most glasshouse ornamentals and food crops, especially fuchsias, peaches, and citrus plants. During hot summers the mites will move outdoors, attacking strawberries, roses, and beans. Leaves dry up and fall off.

Prevention There is no good method of prevention, but if weather conditions permit, regular spraying and misting with water will help deter them. The mites seem to collect near drafts, and if doors and windows are sealed, they seem to build up more slowly.

Control Red spider mites quickly build up resistance to insecticides, and it is necessary to change to a different chemical after a few applications. Spray

every 7-10 days for a few weeks to provide a good control. Biological treatment with the mite *Phytoseiulus persimilis* will be effective if the infestation is light.

Vine weevil

Larvae are creamy white with a brown head, curved, legless, just under $\frac{1}{2}$ in (10 mm) long, and live in the soil. The adults are dull black with antennae bent in the middle. All weevils are female and lay hundreds of eggs in a season.

Attacks Larvae feed on the roots of houseplants and outdoor plants, including rhododendron and primula, causing wilting and even death. They tunnel into the corms of begonias and cyclamens. The adult weevil is more noticeable between spring and fall, feeding at night and eating irregular notches into the leaf margins of euonymus, rhododendron, pieris, and hydrangea.

Prevention None.

Control Insecticides mixed into potting medium offer some control. Biological control using nematodes is effective if they are watered onto warm, moist potting soil in late summer. In open ground the temperature has to be over 60°F (15°C) for this to be effective. In wet or heavy soil, the nematodes die, so the treatment has to be repeated every year.

Absence of soil is no reason not to garden. Pelargoniums, lilies, begonias, roses, and nemesia are all happy growing in containers.

starting points

Undoubtedly, a large number of first-time gardeners move into new houses with a bare canvas for a garden and are going to have fun deciding what type of garden to go for and what feature to put where. Others will opt for an older house with a garden that is in some sort of condition, be it well maintained or in need of a change, and here you can take a bit of time to decide what you are going to do. Some potential gardeners will be young, and others won't be so young. There will be couples with young families and those whose children have children of their own, and at least part of the garden has to be for them and their friends when they visit. Trust me, you are going to enjoy being a gardener, and it will show. Leaving out the extremes of a palace and a tenth-story apartment with a balcony, I have tried to include most of the garden types I've encountered. Follow these ideas to work with what you've got, looking at the hard landscaping before you start adding any plants.

When starting a garden from scratch, clear the area thoroughly and dispose of all trash and debris off site. Retain any larger trees to provide some maturity while you sort out the rest.

new house, vacant plot

It is very easy to despair and want to throw in the towel when faced with a new, raw garden, either bare earth or covered with weeds and a boundary highlighted in concrete posts and wire. A blank canvas and you have never painted before! Let me give you some words of comfort: at least you have nothing to undo, no one else's mistakes to rectify and that will save you time and money.

Clearing up The first job is to find all the gardening gifts that the nice builder has left behind for you. They are usually hidden under the thin layer of topsoil that has been spread like butter over the hard-packed clay subsoil. This in turn was flattened with a digger bucket when the ground was a quagmire. There will be all sorts of trash and debris including bricks, lumber, plywood, shingles, and an area of weak, semihard mortar where the cement mixer was religiously washed out every night.

Remove as much of this debris as possible from the top 10 in (25 cm) of soil and dispose of it off site or in a dumpster, and immediately the whole place will look better.

Dumpster-loads of builders' rubble are a worst-case scenario – many construction firms go out of their way to clear up the site before handover. If the topsoil was stripped and properly stored prior to building, there should be at least as much to be replaced as came off the plot, plus an extra few inches that was originally on the drive and the building plot itself. A polite request and even a friendly smile will probably not get you any extra soil, but holding back the final payment usually guarantees you as much as you need.

What have you got? Your garden may be a bare plot of ground, but it can provide you with a lot of information. We have already discussed types of soil and drainage problems. If you look around, you can identify areas of shade, what is causing them, and the time of day they are shaded. A neighbor's tree may cast a shadow, or part of the garden may simply face away from the sun. You can find which direction your garden faces by noting where the sun is at different times of the day.

What is the boundary to your property made of? Post and wire fences don't do much for a garden. Wooden fences make better boundaries, and it would be great if you happen to have a hedge of some sort.

Perimeter screen

With a new garden, screening for shelter and privacy is a priority. This can be achieved by fencing, walls, or a living screen of trees or shrubs (planting instructions are on page 36). But remember that tall trees or high hedges can shade the garden. If the same type of fence or hedge is used for the entire boundary, the garden can look closed in and monotonous. Relieve it with different materials and types of hedge.

Marking beds

Landscape design cannot be rushed. To give you the time to change your mind and come to a final decision on the location of flowerbeds, fruit garden, and other areas, it is worthwhile sowing the majority of the land with grass, maintaining the lawn until you decide where everything is going to go. You can then mark these out when the grass is established, using a trickle of sand or a hose to shape the bed. New grass is easily killed with glyphosate weedkiller or can be dug over to form a bed. A lawn is a good start and allows the garden to be used and enjoyed while you make up your mind on the overall design.

Shaping beds with a hose allows you to keep changing your mind until you find the look you like.

Hyrdrangeas on each side of the entrance soften the edges of the path and draw you in. In a new garden, well-filled containers provide color while other plants establish themselves.

Up the garden path

A path is one of the first features to be constructed in the garden. It means you can move around the area and transport materials in a wheelbarrow, even in wet conditions. A path should lead somewhere. It can finish at the compost pile or a sundial, but make sure there is something at the end.

Path surfaces can be varied, and materials are often chosen to match a patio surface. A grass path between matching shrub or perennial beds is pleasant, providing there is not too much foot traffic and that you can avoid using it after a period of rain, when it will turn into mud.

Pea gravel is another material that works well, but like all gravels, it tends to move and needs to be edged to keep it in place. A path also needs to be edged when it is lower than the ground on either side — precast plinths, bricks, tiles, or reproduction rope edging can be used. For walks through a woodland area, bark chippings can be used to great effect. Slabs, bricks, tiles, and crazy paving all form interesting, practical surfaces for paths.

An informal gravel path winds through a bog garden, directing the pedestrian past the most interesting plants.

Laying a path Paths should be sited where there is a "desire line" that takes you from A to B. Since every effort should be made to make even a short path interesting, you may go from A to B via C, if C happens to be an interesting bed, unusual plant, or some other feature. A path can head off from the patio or house toward the tool shed, the glasshouse, or the vegetable garden; and while it is effective to run it along the edge of a shrub bed or between double herbaceous beds, it can be designed to cut through a bed using stepping stones, reverting to a path on the other side, which gives added interest. Make the path wide enough that you can take a wheelbarrow and, where space allows, for two people to walk together.

Points to remember

• Perennial weeds must be removed as they appear and before they can get established.

• Where the ground level changes, paths that are used for wheelbarrows should slope up to the higher area — avoid using steps.

• If you don't give stepping stones a proper base, they will sink in the lawn and fill with water after rainfall.

• Lawn grass will grow over the edge of the path and will need to be trimmed back, which is why you need to keep the path at the same level as the lawn.

Hard-surface paths should be constructed to a reasonable specification. They will have to stand a lot of wear and carry wheelbarrow traffic.

• Mark the line of the path with pegs and string, and excavate the top 6 in (15 cm) of soil.

• Then add a 4 in (10 cm) layer of hardcore. You'll need to rent a percussion hammer to consolidate it.

• Set your chosen path surface in a weak concrete mix on top of the hardcore, keeping the surface level.

• Avoid walking on the path until the concrete has set.

• Gravel paths need a similar hardcore base topped with a layer of coarse gravel, then consolidated before the final finer layer of gravel is laid. Don't make the top layer any deeper than 1 in (2 cm), or it will be difficult to walk on.

• Crushed rock gravel is angular and less likely to move under your feet than round gravel; it comes in a large choice of colors and textures depending on where it has been excavated.

Paths and lawns Where the path borders a lawn, the finished path should be at or slightly below the grass level, so the lawn mower can be driven over the path without damaging the blades. Stepping-stone paths through a lawn should be set at the same level as the grass and should be spaced no more than 12 in (30 cm) apart. The stones can be made from flat pieces of natural rock or man-made tiles or slabs. Space them out on the grass to decide the direction the path is going to take and to work out the ideal, most comfortable spacing. When the route has been decided, the stepping stones may be used as templates. Cut around the perimeter of each one, marking the grass in the shape of the step. Remove the grass sod with a sharp spade and make a hole 6 in (15 cm) deep. Fill with 1-2 in (2-5 cm) grade hardcore. Bed the slabs in a weak concrete mix, keeping the finished surface at the same level as the grass or ½ in (1 cm) lower, so the lawn mower can cut over the stepping stones.

Tips for new gardeners

• If you are planning to install a boundary fence or plant a hedge, try to share the cost with your neighbor.

• Dig the ground over in the fall, leaving the rough lumps to be broken down by the winter frost.

• Leyland cypress is a fast-growing evergreen conifer, which is ideal as a screen in parkland or in a large garden where something needs to be blocked out. But if it is not kept well pruned every year, it will grow to 80 ft (25 m) high with a spread of 26 ft (8 m). It is not a suitable plant for a small garden or a lazy gardener.

• Manhole covers are more difficult to conceal in lawn than in a planted area.

Stepping stones also make an informal path, are easy to walk on if closely spaced, and prevent you from treading on new plants.

making over an established garden

I have often looked at a garden and thought that I would have done it differently, and I am quite sure that there are lots of gardens I have landscaped that other designers would have changed. That is the marvelous thing about garden design: there is no absolutely right way, and if you are happy with what you've got, that's fine. But if you are unhappy with your garden, or have just moved in and are dissatisfied with certain areas, then by all means plan to change it. Perhaps it is overcrowded, devoid of color, not suitable for a young family, or just not to your taste. The beauty about an established garden is that you can do a gradual makeover, changing a bit at a time and yet leaving the bulk of the area usable and not looking like a vacant lot.

When long-established plants are being removed, remember that they will have exhausted the soil by using up all the available nutrients. To give the new inhabitants a good start in life, top up the soil with fertilizer and some humus to make it more moisture retentive. About 1 oz (30 g) of general-purpose fertilizer scattered over 1 sq yard (1 sq m) of earth and raked in will do the job. Add well-rotted farmyard manure, old compost, or leaf mold at a rate of a wheelbarrowful to 4 sq yards to bulk up the soil. Provided you are not growing ericaceous plants such as rhododendron, azaleas, and pieris, all of which like acid soil, then spent mushroom compost, which contains small amounts of lime and so is slightly alkaline, can be added.

New roses for old   In areas where old roses have been dug up, don't replant new roses. The soil will be rose sick, causing new stock to do badly and gradually die. If you want to replace just one or two plants, dig out and change the soil to a depth of 18 in (45 cm). Add fresh loamy soil and plant the new roses into that. On a larger scale, it is better to choose a new site for the rose bed.

Repairing paths   Old paths can usually be replaced or resurfaced. Crazy-paved paths are easy and relatively inexpensive to repair: relay the old slabs on a weak mortar base and grout the cracks with mortar. Try to make sure they are all of the same thickness for ease of laying and on a firm, consolidated base – if it was a well-made path, they will have been. Keep the joints close together to reduce the risk of weed seeds germinating in the cracks.

If you want to reposition a path altogether, you will find that the soil below the foundation of the old path is sterile, sour, and suffering from a lack of oxygen. Digging deeply and adding fertilizer and compost will help make the soil usable.

Sprucing up patios   Patios and hard-surfaced areas that have become shabby and green with algae will benefit from cleaning with a pressure hose. Don't use detergent or hot water, as both will damage nearby plants. Weak mortar in the cracks may lift out during cleaning and should be replaced as soon as possible. Try not to disturb mat-forming and ground-cover plants growing in crevices, since their roots will be

Where plants are spreading over a path, they should be cut back before the path disappears. Mature trees and shrubs may grow larger than you want them to be, and should be dealt with before they get out of hand.

1. As this pine grows, it may create a large area of shade. Get an expert in to cut it back.
2. Sage can be pruned hard without suffering ill effects.
3. This *Helianthemum* (rock rose) can be trimmed so it doesn't encroach on the path. Of course, if you don't like it, you can simply remove it altogether.

going far and wide under the hard surface in search of moisture.

Rejuvenating borders Herbaceous beds that are not well maintained quickly become old and tired-looking. But unlike rose beds, they can be dug out and the area cultivated and beefed up with old farmyard manure or compost. Clearing out the bed can be done at any time, but it is easier to identify the perennials when they are growing, and you may find some worth propagating. Dig out every piece of weed you can see and leave the bed without plants over the fall and winter, removing weeds with a garden fork as they appear. Replant in spring as growth is starting. Add a general fertilizer at a rate of 2 oz (60 g) per sq yard at planting time.

Moving established plants to a new position If you have inherited a plant that you like but think is in the wrong place, don't worry. It is possible to move most plants of manageable size, providing you don't damage the roots and the plant doesn't suffer from a loss of water. Full transplanting instructions are on page 38.

An overgrown garden where only the sun can reach the sundial. The buddleia on the left should be pruned hard, and you will need to cut back a lot of unwanted plants before you find the original beds and paths. The *Choisya ternata* to the left of the sundial should be worth saving.

Tip

If a large conifer needs to be removed from a confined space, it is not necessary to dig up the root. Get a tree surgeon to cut the tree at ground level and leave the root in the ground. It won't regrow, although yew will reshoot from the main trunk (these thin stems are easily cut back.)

an overgrown garden in need of an overhaul

Without constant attention, gardens can quickly become overgrown and quite junglelike, with the strongest-growing plants choking out the remainder. I suppose there is some satisfaction in believing that if it was not for gardeners, the whole world would be in a worse mess.

After some pruning and general thinning out of overgrown plants and the removal of weeds, you will soon see light at the end of the garden – and above and around you as well.

Revealing the underlying structure of a garden

• Paths, particularly gravel ones, can quickly disappear under weeds and a coating of dead leaves. Try to identify the main routes and clear them back, removing all the weeds and seedling plants off the path. Dig out perennial plants that are too close to the edge, so the path can be used again. This way, you can be sure that you are not tramping over the original beds, where there may be plants that are worth saving.

• Identify all the bulky, large plants. Find out if they have any particular pruning requirements, their speed of growth, and season of flowering. Then decide if each one gets the thumbs up or the chop. Some plants will be easily identified from books, but it may be necessary to involve an expert for some of the more unusual plants. A landscape contractor or staff from your local garden center may be able to help.

• Seedling trees of ash and sycamore, which quickly colonize a neglected garden, can be removed in winter or early spring by digging them up with a spade. Give them to those with the space for them or take them straight to the dump or bonfire. If they are not removed when they are young, they will grow into huge trees.

• Perennial and annual weeds can be sprayed with glyphosate weedkiller, but take care not to let the chemical come in contact with plants you want to keep. Glyphosate should be applied on a calm, dry day, anytime from late spring until late summer, when the weeds are actively growing. The chemical is translocated through the leaves into the roots, killing the weeds from the bottom up. Follow the manufacturer's instructions and wear protective clothing, including gloves, when using chemicals.

• Overgrown gardens are often home to a mat of ivy over the ground, ivy up the tree trunks, and ivy covering the paths and walls. It is practically impossible to eliminate it, but constant digging, cutting, pulling, and removing will keep it at bay. Repeated applications of glyphosate will have some effect, but you need to add a "sticker" chemical to the mixture; otherwise, the spray runs off the shiny leaves. Ask at your local garden center for advice.

• Berry vines very quickly take over a neglected area, as the tips of the shoots root where they touch the ground. The best way to remove them is by digging them out. Where there is a whole patch of vines and no other plants to worry about, the vines can be cut close to the ground. When new growth appears in spring, spray with a brushwood weedkiller, which kills all shrubby plants. Nettles may be sprayed with glyphosate or dug out, removing as much of the yellow root as possible.

What to do with trees and shrubs By leaving an upper canopy of mature shrubs and trees, you can form a woodland area in the garden where you can grow all those lovely plants that dislike full sun. Start by identifying the shrubs and trees you have. Some shrubs, such as fuchsia, weigela, lavender, and spiraea, are just not worth rejuvenating if they are old and very woody. They are inexpensive to replace and quick growing so, rather than spending a lot of time trying to save your over-mature plants, dig them out and start again.

Examine other ornamental shrubs and trees. Strong shoots that look slightly different from the main plant and are growing from below or at ground level are likely to be suckers. These grow from the roots of the plant that the variety was grafted onto and should be removed before they overpower the tree or shrub. If they are cut at ground level, they will grow again. It is best to pull or tear them off where they join the root. Roses, contorted hazel, viburnum, and witch hazel are all prone to suckering.

Old fruit trees are almost certain to have diseased branches that must be removed and burned. The most noticeable and dangerous disease is canker, which will kill large branches and eventually the complete tree. It is easily seen in winter when there are no leaves on the trees; it causes sunken areas of discolored bark that are cracked, while the surrounding area is swollen. Small infections can be cut out, removing all of the wood that is stained brown, but once the canker circles a branch, it will kill it.

Silver leaf is a fungal disease of plums and cherries. The foliage becomes silvery, and infected branches do not produce leaves the following year. There is no control, but

10 plants that can be pruned hard

Buddleia davidii Prune in spring.

Cornus alba Prune in spring.

Escallonia rubra var. macrantha Prune after flowering in late summer.

Forsythia x intermedia 'Lynwood' Prune in spring after flowering.

Hebe 'Purple Queen' Prune when large in early summer.

Hydrangea macrophylla Prune in early summer.

Rosa rugosa Prune in late summer after flowering.

Sambucus nigra 'Marginata' Prune in late spring.

Ulex europaeus 'Flore Pleno' Prune every two to three years after flowering.

Viburnum tinus Prune in early spring.

you can cut the diseased branch off well below the obviously infected part, which will have a brown stain when cut. You may be lucky, but most infected trees gradually die.

Giving old hedges a new lease on life Old overgrown hedges can be rejuvenated by cutting hard into the old wood and watering and feeding regularly to encourage new growth. It will take a few years to make a good screen, but may be a better option than removing the whole hedge.

Similarly, hedges that have spread sideways and become too wide can be cut back over a two-year period. Cut them hard on one side the first year and on the opposite side the following year, reducing their width by half. In both cases, cut in late spring to encourage some growth before winter. The cut side will look bare until it grows over, but it is still quicker than starting from scratch. Cut all branches on an angle rather than straight across, to allow water to run off the wound and reduce the risk of rot. Hawthorn, laurel, privet, and yew hedges can be cut hard and will produce new shoots from the old wood, but beech and most conifer hedges are reluctant to do so.

Tip

Renting a shredder to chop up all the prunings and plants that have been removed can not only save a lot of time and space, but presents you with an ideal mulch for use on shrub beds to reduce weeding. Avoid shredding diseased wood, which should be burned along with the thicker branches, tree roots, and weeds. The resulting wood ash can be spread on the ground in fall as a source of high-potash fertilizer. Potash will harden up soft growth that has been produced late in the season and would be easily damaged by frost.

Escape through the back gate seems the only option after years of neglect. But two years and a lot of compost later, this simple makeover has led to a garden to be proud of.

1. Only the fuchsia was worth saving.
2. The lawn leads the eye down the garden to a climbing honeysuckle that has taken off over the gate.
3. *Lavandula angustifolia* 'Twickel Purple' and hebes 'Dazzler,' 'Purple Shamrock,' and 'Quicksilver' enjoy the sun in the central bed.
4. Shrubs, including *Buddleia davidii* 'Black Knight,' *Weigela florida* 'Foliis purpureis,' and *Spiraea japonica* 'Anthony Waterer' soften the wall.

keeping a well-maintained garden looking good

General garden maintenance involves weeding, feeding, pruning, and grass cutting. If you can keep on top of these, the garden will at least look neat and the plants won't suffer.

Getting to grips with weeding The person who claims not to have weeds lives in a high-rise building, the Sahara desert, or perhaps thinks of them as plants to be fed and watered. Weeds and their control are dealt with on pages 30-33, but it is reasonable to assume that in a well-maintained garden, most of the weeds will be annual or "soft" weeds that are easily controlled. Try to remove them while they are still small, before they produce a deep root system and especially before they start to set seed. If you are doing this by hand, the job will be a lot easier after a shower of rain when the soil is moist.

On the other hand, it is best to hoe weeds when the ground is dry and no rain is expected, allowing them to wither and die. If the soil is moist, weeds should be removed after hoeing to prevent them from re-rooting into the damp soil and growing away better than ever.

Feeding – keeping a balance It is quite possible to overfeed plants, causing an imbalance of nutrients. As a result, the plant doesn't flower or may have stunted growth or an excess of spindly shoots. Most plants growing in the ground will benefit from a dressing of slow-release fertilizer

such as bonemeal in the planting hole at planting time. Thereafter, they are quite content to send their roots out in search of nutrients. Impoverished soils and heavy clay subsoils can be enriched if the plants are not making satisfactory growth.

Pruning mature plants Pruning is covered more fully on pages 48–51, but the point to remember here is that it promotes growth. With older, established shrubs, pruning is necessary to keep the plant growing or it will go into decline with less flower and foliage. Buddleia has to be cut hard each spring to encourage new growth that flowers the same year – it can produce branches 8 ft (2.4 m) long by summer. Lavender needs to be pruned every year to encourage new growth from the base, or the shoots become woody, producing little growth. Pruning will also keep a plant in shape and keep it under control.

Keeping the lawn in good shape I have a love-hate relationship with grass cutting. It is the most boring repetitive chore in the garden, and the satisfaction of a good job well done soon wears off because the grass starts to grow again before the mower is back in the shed. To keep a lawn looking good, you have to cut it once a week from mid-spring until at least mid-fall, with a couple of cuts during the winter if the weather is suitable.

On the other hand, mowing is a simple operation, requiring little concentration, allowing you to think of more important things. If you are using a walk-behind mower, there is the bonus of a bit of exercise. Regular mowing is less trouble in the long run, as tall grass is hard to cut. If it is wet and long, the machine constantly clogs up with wet grass. Ride-on grass cutters are fun, but not worth buying if you have less than half an acre of lawn all in one piece.

Pruning is necessary to keep many shrubs healthy, but remember that it also promotes growth. In a mature garden you may have to move some plants to give the others enough space.
1. *Rosa* 'Sanders White' (zones 5-9) scrambling over the entrance will need pruning every year.
2. Plants overhanging the path may be cut back, but will probably grow back all the faster.
3. Don't allow other plants to smother the side of the conifer, or the foliage will turn brown.

Gardening isn't just about plants: here, the variety of horizontal and vertical hard surfaces provide as much interest as the choice of colors, textures, and shapes in the planting.

garden features

The wonderful thing about gardening is that it is much more than just plants and soil. There are all the other aspects and disciplines that make gardening and garden design so interesting. Fencing, patio, decking, paths, shed, arbor, and glasshouse – all or some of them have to be allowed for. Then there are seats, sundials, birdbaths, and barbecues. A water feature, play area or compost pile will take up more space, and if they are not all carefully planned and placed, there will be no space in the garden for the plants.

fences and hedges

Wooden fences play an important part in the garden, either as a boundary or to subdivide a section such as the vegetable garden. They can be used to provide shelter or guarantee privacy.

• Sawn boards for vertical fences can be 6 in (15 cm) wide and up to 8 ft (2.4 m) high. Set them on wooden runners with 1 in (2 cm) gaps between the boards, supported on posts.

• The more exposed the site and the more solid the fence, the stronger the support needs to be. In extreme cases, concrete posts are the answer. Where less will do, wooden posts can be concreted into the ground or special metal stakes driven in and the post attached to the metal base.

• All measurements must be exact or panels and precut lumber won't fit. The uprights for the fence must be plumbed with a level, or the finished result will be in and out like a dog's hind leg.

• Sawn boards may also be formed into panels 6 ft (2 m) wide and 3 ft–6 ft (1–2 m) high with boards overlapping horizontally.

• Peeled bark posts can be cut and assembled on site to form rustic trellis fencing for use in cottage gardens to grow climbers up.

A wooden fence softened by foliage and flowers. The poppies make a splash of color.

Points to watch out for

• On sloping ground, the fence will have to be stepped, keeping the posts vertical.

• Keep the base of the fence clear of the ground to prevent the lumber from rotting.

• Use galvanized nails to prevent rust.

• Don't use paints, preservatives, and stains that are not plant friendly.

• On windy sites, don't use solid fences. A solid barrier will stop the wind from filtering through: this causes turbulence on the other side of the fence which is supposedly sheltered.

• Tanalized lumber treated with a preservative will last for years. Apply a combined wood stain and preservative every year to make it look like new and prevent timber rot.

Using diplomacy Erecting boundary fencing can be fraught with problems when there are neighbors involved. If your deeds or tenancy agreement do not specify who is responsible for the boundary, the best option is for both of you to share the cost of the fence and maintain it year about. To keep the peace, it is desirable that the fence is double sided, so it looks attractive from either side.

Fencing within a garden In larger gardens, internal dividing fences can be used to good effect to partition fruit and vegetable plots and to screen unsightly cluttered areas. These fences can be planted with climbers or even trained fruit trees. Where it is not necessary to keep domestic animals out or in, open ranch fencing or rustic trellis may be used and softened with plants. This type of fence around a patio will provide shelter and a level of privacy.

Total privacy and shelter are provided by a dense beech hedge with an arched entrance in the corner.

A level, uniformly dark green, weedfree lawn is a thing of beauty.

thinking about grass

The lawn is a sort of love it, hate it aspect of gardening, and as I've said elsewhere, I love to hate it. Let me tell you the bad news first, and then I will tell you the really bad news. The maintenance of a good-quality lawn takes time, money, and a lot of hard work. Now, by good quality I mean a lawn that is level, without obvious humps, lumps, bumps, hollows, dips, or molehills. It will be uniformly green, not turn yellow in summer and stop short of being sodden wet in winter. Added to this, it will be reasonably free of weeds, especially dandelions, daisies, buttercup, speedwell, and moss. Here I must declare an interest: I have a grass area, and it doesn't fit this description, so I do not call it a lawn. I used to have three grass areas, but I grew up and got a bit of sense.

Lots of people have good lawns, and some have excellent specimens; but even a lawnaholic will have to admit that it takes time. The operations go something like this: edge the grass, spray for weeds, apply lawn sand, spike, feed, scarify, grit the surface, dress, and spray for diseases. Did I forget to mention cutting the grass? Well, no matter, you only have to do it about 26 times from spring until fall, and then a few times in the winter when the weather is suitable. I have seen summers when we have hardly had 26 dry days in total!

Now, it is not my intention to deter you, but I don't want you to opt for a lawn and then be disappointed: a lawn is for life, not just the summer vacation.

Creating a lawn from scratch

Start by preparing the site. Remove any debris, builders' rubble, and large stones that are on the surface, and apply weedkiller such as glyphosate to the foliage of weeds. You need to allow at least four weeks for the chemical to work, and if any perennial weeds reappear during this time, dig them out, making sure to get up every root. Annual weeds need to be hoed off before they set seed.

Dig or rotovate the soil, and level any humps and depressions. If there are large humps, you may need to strip off the topsoil and level the subsoil, before replacing the topsoil and discarding the surplus subsoil.

Finally, rake the surface to level it, checking at regular intervals with a long wooden straightedge and a level. Remove any remaining debris. Apply a general-purpose fertilizer at 1 oz (30 g) per sq yd and tread the surface to firm the soil. Give one final raking to remove the footprints and leave the surface of the soil fine and firm, with no soft areas.

Growing a lawn from seed

Choose a mixture of seed that will produce the type of lawn you need. A mixture for a fine-quality lawn will contain seed of fescue and bent grass. If a hard-wearing lawn is required for a play area, some of the rye grasses will do better. There are special mixtures for dry sites and for light shade under trees.

The condition of the soil and the season have to be considered. It takes very little rain to make the soil surface sticky, and seed should not be sown until the surface dries out. Fall sowing is best if your summers are hot and dry, allowing seed to become established before there is a dry period. A late spring sowing will grow quickly and be well established by late summer.

Tips

• Old grass is usually infested in spring with leatherjackets, the grubs of the crane fly or daddy long-legs, which eat the grass roots. Water the lawn and then cover it overnight with a black plastic sheet. In the morning remove the cover, and all the leatherjackets will have come to the surface in time to make a good breakfast for the birds, especially the starlings.

• When cutting the grass, try to vary the direction of cut each time to catch unawares the flat-growing, weed-type grass that lies down in front of the blades. This will also prevent the mower wheels from constantly running over the same strip of lawn.

The seed should be broadcast over the area at a rate of 1 oz (30 g) per sq yd. If there is a light wind, scatter the seed by hand, with the wind and not against it. If you don't feel confident of sowing at the correct rate, mark the area into yard-wide strips with cord, to help you check. Lightly rake the grass seed into the soil surface, and if it hasn't rained after two days, water using a sprinkler. Warm moist weather will speed up the germination, and the seedling grasses can appear inside two weeks. If the soil is dry or there is a cold period, it can take as long as four weeks before greenness appears. Try to stay off the grass until it is 2 in (5 cm) long. You can then give it its first cut using a rotary cutter set high to just top the grass. Cylinder mowers can't be used at this stage since they tend to pull the new grass and disturb the roots.

Laying sod

Although sod is expensive, the effect is practically instant. The ideal time to lay sod is early fall to late spring, providing the soil conditions are workable and the surface isn't wet or muddy and there is no frost on the ground or expected until the sod is laid.

Prepare the site in the same way as for sowing grass, with the surface fine, level, and firm. Choose a grade of sod to suit the level of work and play the grass will have to tolerate. As with grass seeds, there are different qualities of sod available, including top-quality fine grasses fit for a tennis court and hard-wearing mixtures for family use. The sod will be delivered rolled up, and it is essential that it is laid as soon as possible to prevent it from drying out. If it has to be kept overnight, store the rolls under cover in an airy place protected from rain.

Overleaf: The lawn sets off the plants, and plants highlight the lawn.

When laying sod, it is essential to work from the grass that has already been laid and not on the bare earth. Stand on a plank to distribute your weight and avoid damaging the sod. Roll the grass out in a straight line and butt the second sod tightly to the first. Sod is supplied with only a thin layer of soil and is easily damaged if it is not carried carefully. The second row of sod is laid like a second layer of bricks in a wall, so that the joints are not in line with the joints in the first row. Firm the row of sod with the back of a metal rake, move the plank over, and repeat until the area is covered. After the sod is laid, water regularly if there is no rain. After four weeks, the roots will have anchored the sod to the soil. You can start to cut the new lawn as soon as the grass is long enough. Cracks may appear if the sod was not laid tightly, but they can be filled with a peat/soil mixture brushed into the grass.

Initial lawn care Water as necessary in periods of hot, dry weather and cut the grass on a regular basis, gradually lowering the height of the mower blades to cut the grass shorter. But don't scalp the grass, as close-cut lawns are more prone to being colonized by moss. Weeds will appear, especially in lawns grown from seed, but don't apply weedkillers for at least six months – this will allow the grass time to become established. Avoid using high-nitrogen fertilizers for the same length of time, because it is more important for the grass plants to build up strong root systems than to produce a lot of leaf (which nitrogen would encourage).

Cutting the grass Deciding which way to cut the grass is the first hurdle. You have a range of options from small push mowers that are hard work, through to

An uneven application of fertilizer will result in the overdosed areas being scorched or killed.

pedestrian-operated rotary and cylinder cutters, where you walk behind a machine that is power driven by gas, battery, or electricity. Then there are hover cutters that float on a cushion of air rather than on wheels.

Rotary mowers do not leave as fine a cut as cylinder cutters. With rotaries, the blades rotate parallel with the grass surface, whereas cylinder blades spin down toward the grass and are close together, resulting in a finer cut with the grass finely chopped up. Mulching mowers literally chop up the grass to a fine mulch that can stay on the lawn and will disappear into the surface.

There are several schools of thought on the subject of grass cuttings, but the most popular advice is to leave the cuttings on the lawn after the first cut and again after the last cut of the season. In between they can either be collected in the grass box and removed or left on the lawn. If the clippings are being removed, you will need a dumping area out of sight. If they are being used in the compost pile, only thin layers of about 4 in (10 cm) can be added at any one time or they won't rot down properly.

Try to choose a machine whose height of cut can be adjusted. It is advisable not to cut too low at the start of the season or during very dry weather. The recommended height will depend on the type of grass, as some varieties can tolerate closer cutting than others, but as a rough guide ½ in (1.5 cm) to 1 in (2.5 cm) is fine in summer.

A roller at the rear of the grass cutter produces the light and dark green stripes beloved by all and reminiscent of a football field. As you walk up and down, the roller flattens the grass in opposite directions and the light shines on the flat blades. If the grass was all rolled in the same direction, there would be no shading.

Rejuvenating an old lawn
It is amazing what you can do with an old overgrown, weedy grass area that used to be a lawn. If the site is level, half your battle is won. In spring, summer, or early fall, rough cut with a rotary mower or use a strimmer to remove most of the long grass, raking it off and cutting again until you get it to about 3–4 in (8–10

Plantain and daisies will soon smother the finer grasses if you don't keep them under control.

cm) high. Let the grass recover and start growing again, and then apply a selective lawn weedkiller to kill a broad range of grass weeds, following the manufacturer's directions. It is better to target weeds rather than spread weed killer across the lawn. After a few days, cut the grass again and give it an application of lawn fertilizer to encourage growth. If you require a first-class lawn, you have just wasted your time, but if you will settle for a level, green, reasonably weedfree grass area that looks good, you have probably just achieved it.

Weeding and feeding Whenever the subject of lawns crops up, you will hear the words "weed and feed" used together. The grass is treated for weeds, and at the same time it is fed with a high-nitrogen fertilizer. Weeds growing strongly from the application of fertilizer are softer and so are more easily killed with the selective weedkiller that attacks weeds without damaging the grass. The grass benefits from the fertilizer and quickly fills the space left by the dead weeds.

planning a patio

A patio is like a room outdoors, and when the weather is suitable, it can be used for relaxation, entertaining, and eating. Essentially, it is an area of level hard surface in the garden where you can sit in sun or shade with table and chairs and, hopefully, enjoy the surroundings. The surface may be gravel, crazy paving (broken paving slabs), concrete slabs, pre-formed tiles, bricks, or natural slate or stone. The entire area may be enclosed by planted beds, or the patio can be raised above the surrounding garden, reached by steps up from a lawn or path.

Having the patio as an extension to the house is ideal for enjoying a cup of coffee and a quick look at the paper before work. The main factor when choosing the site is sun. A sunless site is to be avoided at all cost: it will be cold, and the patio surface will turn green through lack of light, which encourages algae to grow.

There is no good reason for having just one patio, and if you have space, a second area away from the house at the end of a path, through lawn or shrubbery, will give you a choice of places to sit. While the patio should be in a sunny position, it is useful to have a section shaded for use when the sun gets too hot or where things can be kept cool. A wooden arbor covering part of the patio and draped in climbers will provide the shade required. The sound and sight of running water add to the idyllic image, and why not finish off with two birch trees 10 ft (3 m) apart to cast some shade and to swing a hammock from!

Laying the foundations

• It is essential that a patio is laid on a firm foundation and that surface water can run off. Start by excavating to a depth of 8 in (20 cm) below the finished level — keep the topsoil for use elsewhere. This is the chance to drain areas that are damp (using the method on page 23), but don't try to make a patio on very wet ground.

• Form a layer of clean 2 in (5 cm) stone 4 in (10 cm) deep and consolidate it using a percussion hammer (which you can rent from some garden centers).

• Lay a layer of landscape fabric on top to prevent weeds from growing up, and surface with a 2 in (5 cm) layer of vibrated sand.

• Create a very slight slope so water will run off the surface. A gradient of 1 in in 6 ft (25 mm in 1.8 m) sloping away from the house walls is adequate. Using a straight-edge and a level to guarantee accuracy, drive in wooden stakes 6 ft (1.8 m) apart, with each stake 1 in (25 mm) lower than the one before. Make sure there are no depressions in the vibrated sand between the stakes, so you have an evenly sloping surface. Then remove the stakes and lay your chosen surface on the sand. Bricks and tiles should be laid tight together and fine dry sand brushed into the gaps and vibrated. Slabs and crazy paving need to be grouted with a very wet mix of four parts cement and one part sand brushed into the joints. Brush off excess mortar the following day. When old stone is being laid, there is usually a difference in the thickness of the pieces, and it may be necessary to bed each piece individually on a fairly weak, dry mortar mix of four parts sand to one part cement.

Roses drape a rustic arch leading into the patio.

Points to watch out for

• Over time, the surface of sandstone slabs will flake off in layers and will be made worse by frost action.

• If the patio is next to a wall, leave holes in the surface at the base of the wall for climbing plants.

• Iron containers will rust and stain the patio surface.

• Make the patio big enough to accommodate furniture and guests.

• Make any steps from the patio to the garden from the same material to give continuity.

Wisteria drapes a wooden arbor. Wisteria needs to be pruned after flowering and again in late winter. The effort is rewarded by a glorious display of flowers and beautiful fragrance, followed in late summer and fall by velvety pods.

arbor

An arbor is an open wooden structure tall enough to stand under and ideal for supporting climbing plants. It is often built in the form of an arch or as an open roof over a patio. For a large arbor the lumber can be rustic peeled bark poles, or cut lumber as bulky as possible, with cross beams of equal size. Smaller structures can be made of lighter materials, such as wrought iron or wooden latticework, but remember that some materials will require more maintenance than others. Wood needs staining or preserving; metal should be treated for rust.

Where an arbor is used to shade a patio, uprights must not obstruct the main area of the patio. You will need substantial beams, so make sure they are well concreted into the ground and that the cross beams are at least 8 ft (2.5 m) above ground level to allow plants to grow over the bars without trailing down at head height. Choose climbers that look interesting for a good part of the year with leaf, flower,

and fruit. Grapevines perform well and provide edible fruit in mild climates, and wisteria, if pruned and trained, will be a mass of flowers during late spring and early summer.

Points to watch out for

• Form recessed joints where the vertical posts meet the cross bars and use galvanized nails that won't rust.

• Use well-seasoned wood to avoid the lumber from warping and splitting.

• When concreting the posts into the ground, leave space for planting climbers and provide galvanized or plastic mesh support to get the plants growing up and over the top.

• When making an arch over a path, position the uprights at least 24 in (60 cm) away from the sides of the path, to allow room for plants to grow up without blocking the way through.

play area

If you are creating a separate area for children to play in, site it close to the house where it can be clearly seen. A see-through fence, such as split stakes spaced apart and wired together, will allow anyone supervising to at least blink without having the children disappear.

Grass is an ideal play surface in summer, but in winter it will become churned up into mud very quickly. An area of ½ in (13 mm) diameter around gravel may be hard on bare feet, but at least it is dry and mudfree underfoot. Bark mulch spread 4 in (10 cm) deep will cushion falls and is ideal where there are no dogs or cats to use it as a toilet area.

Play equipment needs to be well spaced out with nothing immediately behind or in front of a swing, for obvious reasons. Where upright posts of swings, jungle gyms, etc., are concreted into the ground, the concrete should be 6 in (15 cm) below the soil surface and covered with soil or mulch. Outdoor sand boxes are always popular. They need to be free draining, with a base that can be brushed clean when changing the sand. A lightweight cover will keep animals out when the box is not in use. Any shrubs planted in the area must be able to withstand a bit of abuse and be free of thorns and spines. Plants such as buddleia, the butterfly bush, can tolerate a lot of damage. Broken branches will serve as a form of crude pruning, which is just what this shrub needs every year.

A playhouse in the area can be used to shelter in if a shower comes up and is a useful place to store the toys that can't stay outside permanently.

If the garden is too small to subdivide, allow the children free range. Encourage them to help with the whole garden and to remove their toys to make way for the lawn mower.

Lawns are an ideal site for jungle gyms, but placing matting or coarse bark around the base will provide softer landings.

garden ornaments

Garden seat Larger gardens can accommodate more than one seat. Position some in sun and some in shade, to take in views of special parts of the garden. They come in all shapes and materials, including stone, hardwood, rustic lumber, and plastic, but have at least one that is comfortable to the point that you can doze off on it without getting numb. In winter you may want to bring one or two under cover.

Birdbath A birdbath is another permanent fixture, and every garden should have one. It doesn't have to be elaborate, and provided it is shallow, the birds will use it. Position it where it can be seen from the house, and you will get hours of enjoyment as birds bathe and drink, but don't forget to keep it topped up with water!

Garden furniture can be both practical and ornamental, so whether you choose to sit in the sun or the shade, position your seating so you can delight in the scent of nearby shrubs.

A birdbath makes a focal point. Site it so you can see it from the house and enjoy the activity of the birds.

Sundial A sundial usually stays out all year, and the only rule to be observed is that it should be in full sun all day long. You'll probably never use it, but there is always one visitor who wants to tell the time and thinks he knows how to read the dial.

Points to watch out for

• More and more garden ornaments are being stolen each year: secure with a bolt and chain attached to a permanent stake all those that are left outside.

• Full sun will bleach hardwood seats over a period of time. Give them a little protection and oil them lightly each spring with linseed oil.

• It is hard to mow grass around the base of ornaments. Set them on a hard surface that is flush with the grass.

• Plastic summer furniture will blow all over the place if it is left out in windy weather and is sure to damage your prize plants. Anchor it to the ground or store it under cover when not in use.

water features

No garden should be without one of these. The sound and sight of moving water is all things to all people. It is relaxing, interesting, fascinating, and above all rewarding if you have done the work yourself. Features can range from little trickles to a crashing crescendo tumbling over rocks like whitewater and down a waterfall into a pool of flowering plants and darting fish.

Large or small, if the water feature can be seen and heard from parts of the garden in summer and from the house in winter, it more than earns its space in the garden. Birds will bathe in shallow pools and frogs breed in the pond, and knowing that both reduce the slug and snail population is more than a bonus.

Small water features can be purchased in kit form complete with a submersible pump and ready to install. A wall-mounted lion's head spouting water into a bowl below or a miniature fountain depositing water onto round cobblestones or trickling over a circular stone will sit neatly on the smallest patio and make you feel cooler on a hot day.

Constructing a water feature is a serious undertaking. Unlike many other garden projects, where there is a bit of latitude and a few mistakes can be made without having much effect, a water feature has to be 100 percent perfect. Water is very unforgiving, and if levels are not exactly right, or the flow is too fierce or, worst of all, if there is a leak, the whole job may have to be redone from scratch.

Plants around a pond not only create interest and soften the edges; by shading the water, they also reduce the risk of algae.

Building a pond Ponds are easier to construct if the soil and subsoil are not too difficult to dig. It's a good idea to check with a few test holes that you won't hit rock just below the surface. It is also an advantage to have a level site. On a sloping site the low side has to be built up to keep the top of the pond at the same level. But if you have a flat site at the base of a slope, you have a ready-made location for a waterfall. All you need is a small upper pond or an outlet between rocks for the water to be pumped up to, then it can flow down to the bottom pond. Where there is no suitable slope or high ground, the soil dug out to make the pond can be piled up to provide height close by.

Lining the pond It is important to decide early in the process what material you are going to use to form the pond. You have several options.

• In some areas, the local clay is suitable for coating the sides and the base. If the pond is kept full of water so the clay doesn't dry out, it will act as a seal.

• Concrete can be used to line the pool if there is no settlement of the ground, which would cause it to crack. Coat the dry concrete with a waterproofing sealant, painting it on before the pond is filled with water.

• Molded preformed rigid liners of fiberglass are strong and virtually indestructible. They are made in different shapes and sizes, and you can add sections to form waterfalls and cascades with molded edges to give the appearance of rocks.

• Liners are available in different qualities, from cheap plastic that may last for a few years to heavy duty vinyl and butyl, guaranteed to last anything from 20 years to a lifetime. The advantage of using a liner is that you can decide the shape and size, including depth, of the pond.

• When a liner is being used, the base and sides of the hole must be firm and able to withstand the weight of the water, which will be considerable. Bed the liner on a 2 in (5 cm) layer of fine sand or underfelt to prevent small sharp stones from puncturing it. When working in the pond on a flexible liner, remove your shoes or at least clean them, in case there are stones embedded in the soles.

The ideal depth A pond can be shallow or deep, but a deep pond is more difficult to clean out: 30–36 in (75–90 cm) is a good depth for fish and plants, combined with a couple of shallow shelves at the sides at a depth of 8–18 in (20–45 cm) to allow for plants that like shallow water, such as the white bog arum *Calla palustris* (zones 4-8) and two striking irises, *Iris laevigata* (zones 4-9), which has blue flowers, and *I. versicolor*, whose violet flowers have purple veins and a hint of gold.

The sides can slope gently, but not too much or the liner becomes obvious. While the pond is filling, keep the liner taut to avoid wrinkles. If the sides are curved, fold the liner into neat pleats that the water will hold in place.

Don't be tempted to trim off the surplus liner at the edges until the pond is full, and leave an overlap of 12 in (30 cm) all around the top. A pond may be surrounded with grass or planted up to the edge with plants such as primula, hosta, and iris, which will be reflected in the water. If you plan to lay a border for walking on, it will have to be firm, secure, and smooth, to prevent any risk of falling in. Lay paving slabs, tiles, slate, or flat stones on top of the liner on a bed of wet mortar. Arrange them so they overhang the edge of the pond by 2 in (5 cm) to hide the liner above water level.

Streams and waterfalls Miniature streams and waterfalls linked to a pond can be made using a liner in exactly the same way as the pond. The sides need only be deep enough to hold the flow of water. The breadth of the

Construct a pond carefully using good-quality materials and it will last a lifetime.

Slabs overhanging edge of pond

Ledge for plants that enjoy shallow water

Flexible liner

Fine sand or underfelt

stream determines the speed the water flows: narrow gorgelike streams flow fast, while the water in broad, unimpeded areas moves smoothly.

Where separate liners meet, for example, where a stream joins a pond, the two liners need to have a generous overlap. The liner carrying the water down has to overhang the pond liner, to allow the water to flow into the pond. If the stream liner is under the pond liner, the water will run below the liner and eventually drain the pond.

Installing a pump   The most popular type of pump is the submersible version, placed in the bottom of the pond. To create a waterfall, the water is pumped up through a flexible hose buried in the soil nearby. The hose should have as large a diameter as possible. The outlet can be disguised among rocks, or it can feed into a top pond that then overflows down toward the source and the water is circulated back up. A fountain may be incorporated into the feature, but take care that during windy weather the spray doesn't blow out of the pond and cause the level to drop.

There is always the worry of young children falling into the pond, so if this is a possibility, cover the surface of the pond with wire. A shallow pond can be filled to the brim with cobblestones that change color when wet. A fountain can operate through the stones and looks intriguing – where is the water coming from and going to?

Water and well-worn rock make a great combination. In this Australian garden, the half-hardy purple agapanthus is happy outside.

Points to watch out for

• Water and electricity don't mix. Always employ a qualified electrician to connect the pump and use special outdoor cable to run the power from the house. Bury the cable 24 in (60 cm) deep in a trench, with yellow plastic tape over the cable warning of live electricity.

• If you are installing outside lights at the same time as a pump, they will have to be wired separately, since the pump will be used during the day when the lights aren't needed.

• Remember where hoses are buried so you don't stick a garden fork through them.

• Algae and green water will form if there is no movement of water or if the pond is in full sun. A fountain or waterfall will keep the water moving, and if part of the pond is shaded by plants, the problem won't be as bad.

• Site a pond away from deciduous trees, since the leaves tend to blow into the pond in the fall. If you don't clear the leaves out, they produce a gas as they rot down which is harmful to fish, plus they clog up pump filters.

• Where water flows into a pond from a stream, direct it over a flat rock that overhangs the pond. The falling water will cause more of a splash.

• Let a new pump run for 24 hours, keeping a regular watch to make sure your feature is not losing water. Never let the pump run without water or it will overheat.

atmosphere at a time when you are trying to keep humidity levels low. Fan heaters that can be reversed to blow cold air will be useful in summer when temperatures tend to be too high.

Putting a glasshouse to good use
I have referred earlier to growing edible crops under glass, and while it is not easy to grow different crops in the same area, it can be successful if care and attention is given to hygiene. Some plants will require higher temperatures, and others will need more water and humidity at a time when you are trying to keep the foliage of some dry. But if plants are widely spaced, it can still work. You will need to use as much ventilation as possible to get air moving through the house, and on sunny days, the door can be left open. Plants that do better in the glasshouse soil may be planted on one side, while those in pots and growbags can be positioned on the opposite side. Keep a close watch for pests, which will spread rapidly in an enclosed environment. Aphids are particularly hard to control. Diseases may attack the roots, stems, leaves, and fruit: if in doubt, dump any sick or suspect plants rather than risk losing all of your crops.

What to grow
Having decided on the type of glasshouse, the site, and equipment, you must now decide what to grow. The controlled environment of a glasshouse allows you to succeed with plants that would not survive outside. You can also consider a range of plants that do well when grown without protection, but that do even better under cover and, in the case of fruit such as strawberries, crop earlier at a time when they are expensive to buy. In cooler climates, permanent glasshouse plants include edible crops such as peaches, grapes, and figs, planted directly into the soil and grown up the wall and over the roof. Annual crops include tomato, cucumber, corn on the cob, peppers, and eggplant – all of which can be raised from seed or purchased as small plants.

A colorful display, including begonias, fuchsias, and geraniums, flourishes under glass.

What to grow in a greenhouse

Homegrown tomatoes

The flavor of your own tomatoes is a thing to be marveled at. Compared to commercially grown fruit purchased in a store, the taste is so much better. They are an easy crop to grow, and while mistakes can be made, and in a poor season pests and diseases may claim some plants, there are usually more than enough tomatoes to feed you, your friends, and the neighbors.

Tomatoes can be raised from seed, but it is easier to buy them as young plants from garden centers, all ready for planting out. Because of their popularity, there is a good selection of varieties available.

In a frostfree glasshouse, plants can be started off as early as mid March, and you may be picking tomatoes in late May.

How to grow

• If the glasshouse soil is new and has never cropped tomatoes or potatoes (potatoes are in the same family as tomatoes and suffer from similar diseases), I would grow the tomatoes in the soil. Incorporate lots of compost or old farmyard manure before planting and a base dressing of 2 oz (60 g) of a balanced general purpose fertilizer per sq yd. Water the soil before planting and try not to give much more water until the first fruit are starting to swell.

• Where crops have been grown before or where the floor of the house is paved, they can be planted in pots or in growbags – bags of soilless medium with added nutrients. Lay the bag flat, cut holes in the plastic, and put the plants into the medium. Most bags are marked for three planting holes, but if you have enough space in the glasshouse, two plants to a bag will give better results.

• Tomato plants need to be supported as they grow. Attach a length of soft string to a wire running along the inside of the roof. Tie the other end loosely to the base of the plant and twist the string around the stem as the plant grows. Trusses of yellow flowers will appear, and shortly after they will be replaced by young green fruit.

Watering and feeding on a regular basis is essential. By the time the third truss of fruit has appeared, they will be using up to 8 pt (4 liters) of water every other day. Each plant will provide 6–11 lb (3–5 kg) of fruit.

Varieties to grow

Varieties come and go with dozens of new "improved" ones each year. If you are growing for flavor, these varieties are worth trying.

Gardeners' Delight Small cherry-sized tomatoes with a tangy taste.

Alicante Produces early crops of well-flavored medium-sized fruit.

Sungold The orange fruit is bite-sized and produced over a long period into late fall.

Moneymaker An old variety that is still popular and easy to grow, with reasonable flavor and medium-sized fruit.

Cool cucumbers

This is another easy-to-grow crop, and the results justify taking that extra little bit of trouble. Like tomatoes, cucumbers can be grown from seed or purchased as young plants. Choose an all-female variety that won't produce male flowers: fertilized cucumbers are bitter.

• Grow the plants in growbags (two per bag) or in large pots, at least 12 in (30 cm) in diameter, in a rich, free-draining medium. Keep the soil moist at all times, but don't allow it to become waterlogged.

• Train the plants in a similar way to tomatoes using string to support them. Check them every day as cucumbers grow very quickly. The fruit is produced at the leaf axils, so remove all the side shoots and any fruit that forms on the bottom 24 in (60 cm) of the plant.

• Provide lots of ventilation, and wet the path or floor on warm sunny days to encourage a moist atmosphere.

• Once the first fruits have started to swell, feed with a high potash tomato feed every week. Pick the fruits as they ripen. An average plant will produce between six and 10 good-sized fruits.

Varieties to grow
(Not found in Canada)

Aidas An all-female variety with smooth-skinned fruit, suitable for growing in an unheated glasshouse.

Petita Lots of small fruit with a good flavor.

Kyoto A Japanese type that is really easy to grow.

Warning

Even the all-female varieties can produce an occasional male flower, especially if the plant is under stress. Female flowers are easily recognized; they have a miniature cucumber behind the yellow flower; the male flowers merely have a thin stalk.

Corn on the cob

Corn is one of those crops that is best eaten immediately after picking. The sugar content very quickly converts to starch, and even one hour will make a difference to the flavor.

• Grow them from seed or buy plants. They will grow in a cold glasshouse either in large pots or in the soil, but they don't like to be disturbed, so plant them before they become pot bound. Plant 18 in (45 cm) apart and don't allow the roots to dry out at any stage.

• The silky brown tassel at the top of the plant is the male flower and should be gently shaken daily to assist pollination. On average, each plant will produce one or two good cobs.

Varieties to grow

Royal Sweet Golden yellow kernels and very sweet, this variety will tolerate cooler conditions and produces 7 in (18 cm) cobs.

Honey Bantam Bicolour This variety has a mixture of yellow and creamy white kernels and is very sweet. It matures early with 7 in (18 cm) cobs.

Tip

It is important that the cobs are picked as soon as they are ripe. When the silks (the tuft of threads at the end of the cob) have turned brown, peel back part of the sheath that surrounds the kernel. Squeeze a couple of the grains: if the liquid is watery, the cob is not ripe. If the liquid is creamy, the cob is ready to pick; but if the grain exudes a thick doughy mass, it is past its best. Don't cut the cob, but twist it off the stem.

Melons

There is no reason why you can't grow melons that have a flavor every bit as good as imported fruit.

• Grow melons in exactly the same way as cucumbers, either raised from seed or as bought plants. Plant two per growbag and don't firm the plants in. Plant them at the same depth as they were in the pots or slightly raised above the soil. Water the plants to settle them in, but avoid watering the leaves or stems.

• Melons grown along the ground will be more vulnerable to slug and snail attacks. Support the fruit off the ground using a handful of straw or pieces of slate. Ideally, grow them up and along wires, set 12 in (30 cm) apart. Train main stems along these wires and remove the growing tip after five leaves. Fruit develops on the side shoots.

• Unlike cucumbers, melons have to be pollinated, so don't remove the male flowers. Once a small fruit has formed, stop the side shoot two leaves beyond it. Thin the fruit to a maximum of five per plant, to make sure they swell to a reasonable size. Net the individual melons using an old pair of tights or a hairnet to support them.

Varieties to grow
(Not found in Canada)

Charmel This form of Charentais melon is fast growing and has a deep orange, sweet flesh with a wonderful aroma.

Sweetheart An early cropper, ideal for growing in an unheated glasshouse.

Tip

It can be difficult to know when melons are ripe. One way is to smell them, and if they have that unmistakable melon aroma, they are ready to eat. If you press gently at the tip, it should be slightly soft.

Eggplant

Eggplants are a talking point in the glasshouse as well as on the table, especially when you point out that they are homegrown. Eggplants are as easy to grow as tomatoes and take up less space. They can be purchased as young plants or grown from seed, but the seed needs to be sown in late February in a propagator at a temperature of 70°F (20°C). Set out two plants per growbag and stake them. When the plant is 12 in (30 cm) high, nip out the growing tip to encourage the plant to become bushy. Feed weekly with a tomato fertilizer once the fruit start to form. Eggplants should be picked while the skin is still shiny. Under good conditions, a plant will be capable of growing five eggplants. Once they have started to swell, the remainder of the flowers should be removed.

Varieties to grow

Black Prince Crops early and produces large fruit.
Moneymaker Early fruiting. Crops well with good flavor.

Capsicum (peppers)

There are two types of peppers: sweet and hot – and some of the hot can be very hot. They are easy to grow; just follow the method for eggplant. Frequent spraying with water will help pollination and reduce the spread of red spider mite, which is a serious pest of peppers. Depending on variety, one plant can produce up to 40 fruit.

Varieties to grow

Big Bertha One of the largest sweet peppers, it will produce fruit 10 in (25 cm) long and crops early.

Thai Dragon This variety should carry a warning. The carrot-shaped shiny red fruit are 4 in (10 cm) long, and just one plant will produce enough hot peppers for all your needs.

Strawberries

It is not that you can't grow perfect strawberries outside in the garden, but when they are grown in a glasshouse, they ripen much earlier in the season. It is advisable to buy certified stock of strawberry runners that are guaranteed to be free of disease: look for well-rooted plants as early in the fall as possible. Pot the plants into a soil-based medium and leave them outside in a sheltered position until midwinter. Bring them into the glasshouse and keep them watered without any feeding until they flower. Pollinate the flowers with a soft brush, moving it gently from one flower to another to transfer pollen and to help fruit production. Give as much ventilation as possible to reduce the risk of gray mold. The plants will start to crop in mid spring, two months before those grown outside. If the light is good, one plant will yield 8 oz (240 g) fruit.

Varieties to grow
(Not found in Canada)

Royal Sovereign Certified stock of this old variety is sometimes hard to come by, but it has superb flavor.
Elvira The large, conical fruit crop well with a very good flavor.

Eggplant, tomatoes, corn, peppers, and strawberries, all fresh from the garden. Even those fruit and vegetables that grow perfectly well outdoors have an extended season, thanks to the protected environment of the glasshouse.

The right plants for the right place: this geometric foliage is the perfect foil for the stark shapes and strong colors of the house behind it. Notice the mulch around the plants, which allows each specimen to stand on its own without the spaces in between being smothered in weeds.

plants for special places

There are fussy plants and others that will put up with whatever conditions they have to face, but even the unfussy have preferences and will show their unhappiness through stunted growth, discolored foliage, and a lack of flowers and fruit. If your soil and climate are average, with no extremes, you are very fortunate and will be able to grow a wide variety of plants with only the very particular refusing to thrive. When you become familiar with your garden, you choose the most suitable plants for the conditions you are able to provide. The plants I have suggested for each location are everyday varieties that are tried and tested. I have also slipped in one that is a "bit more exotic" to give you the edge over the Joneses, especially if they profess to be expert gardeners who know their onions.

Plants for full sun

Many of the plants we grow in full sun are plants that enjoy Mediterranean conditions, where the sun and the heat are complemented by light, sandy, or stony free-draining soil. Choose the warmest, most sheltered site, and if necessary, provide the plants with protection from frost and cold winds.

---

top ten

Anthemis tinctoria 'E. C. Buxton' Perennial

Cerastium tomentosum (snow in summer) Perennial

Diascia rigescens Perennial

Geranium endressii. Perennial

Gleditsia triacanthos 'Sunburst' Deciduous tree

Helianthemum 'Raspberry Ripple' Evergreen shrub

Hordeum jubatum Herbaceous perennial

Juniperus chinensis 'Kuriwao Gold' Conifer

Phlomis fruticosa (Jerusalem sage)

five more to try

Campanula persicifolia Herbaceous perennial

Carpenteria californica Evergreen shrub

Euphorbia characias subsp. *wulfenii* Evergreen shrub

Fremontodendron californicum Evergreen shrub

Gypsophila paniculata Herbaceous perennial

a bit more exotic

Campsis x *tagliabuana* 'Mme Galen' Vigorous climber

Full details of all these plants can be found in the directory on pages 178–189

Plants for shade

It is easy to appreciate a bit of shade when you see the scorch damage that full sun is capable of. But there are some types of shade with accompanying soil that plants are less happy in. Dense shade caused by evergreen trees, combined with large drips of rain from the leaves, an impoverished soil, and a mat of tree roots is, at best, tolerated by some plants. The cold shade on the sunless side of a tall building is often made worse by a chilly draft tunneled around the corners of the walls. Wet shaded sites also restrict the choice of plants. The following species will succeed where others give up.

---

top ten

Crinodendron hookerianum (lantern tree) Evergreen shrub

Daphne laureola (spurge laurel) Evergreen shrub

Euonymus fortunei 'Emerald Gaiety' Evergreen shrub

Hedera colchica 'Dentata Variegata' (Persian ivy) Evergreen climber

Hosta 'Big Daddy' Herbaceous perennial

Lamium maculatum Evergreen perennial

Pachysandra terminalis Evergreen perennial

Skimmia japonica 'Wakehurst White' Evergreen shrub

Tolmiea menziesii (piggyback plant) Herbaceous perennial.

Vinca major 'Variegata' (periwinkle) Evergreen shrub.

five more to try

Aucuba japonica Evergreen shrub

Dicentra formosa Herbaceous perennial

Fatsia japonica Evergreen shrub

Sarcococca confusa Evergreen shrub

Viola labradorica Evergreen perennial

a bit more exotic

Rhodotypos scandens Deciduous shrub

A shady bed overhung by a mature beech tree.

Plants for sandy soil

Sandy soils are quick to warm up and free draining, but in a season with low rainfall they will need irrigating. Mulch with compost, bark, or a deep layer of gravel to conserve moisture in the soil. Suitable plants adapt to the desertlike conditions by sending their roots far and wide and deep in search of water. Feeding them with a liquid foliar drench is quick-acting and reduces the risk of nutrients leaching away. Loose sandy or gritty soil is easily blown around by the wind and can cut off seedlings and young plants at soil level or abrade their stems.

top ten

Brachyglottis monroi Evergreen shrub
Callistemon citrinus (crimson bottlebrush)
    Evergreen shrub
Calluna vulgaris 'Darkness' Evergreen shrub
Dorycnium hirsutum Deciduous shrub
Echinops bannaticus 'Taplow Blue'
    Herbaceous perennial
Eryngium bourgatii Herbaceous perennial
Lespedeza thunbergii Deciduous sub-
    shrub
Limonium platyphyllum (sea lavender)
    Herbaceous perennial
Romneya coulteri (tree poppy)
    Deciduous subshrub
Santolina chamaecyparissus (cotton
    lavender) Evergreen shrub

five more to try

Acanthus hirsutus Herbaceous
    perennial'
Agastache foeniculum Perennial
Artemisia 'Powis Castle' Evergreen
    perennial
Indigofera amblyantha Deciduous shrub
Linum narbonense Herbaceous perennial

a bit more exotic

Ceratostigma willmottianum Deciduous
    shrub

Berberis darwinii is evergreen and spiny, with dark orange flowers in spring. These berries are the autumn display.

Plants for clay soil

A heavy clay soil is every gardener's nightmare — sticky when wet, and hard and cracked when dry. Improving the drainage and opening the soil by incorporating lots of grit and organic matter will help, as will avoiding cultivating the soil when it is wet. If deep mulches are applied annually, the surface rooting area will be improved. In its favor, clay soil is well supplied with nutrients, including trace elements. There is a whole range of plants that can be successfully grown in heavy clay. When planting, fork up the bottom of the planting hole so the roots of the plant can penetrate the clay subsoil more easily and water can also drain away quickly. If you don't do this, the hole becomes a sump and the plant roots get waterlogged.

top ten

Aster novae-angliae 'Harrington's Pink'
    Deciduous perennial
Berberis darwinii Evergreen shrub
Chaenomeles × *superba* (Japanese quince)
    Deciduous shrub
Choisya ternata (Mexican orange
    blossom) Evergreen shrub
Cotoneaster frigidus 'Cornubia' Semi-
    evergreen shrub
Monarda 'Cambridge Scarlet' (bergamot)
    Herbaceous perennial
Potentilla fruticosa Deciduous shrub
Pulmonaria saccharata (lungwort,
    Jerusalem sage) Evergreen perennial
Sambucus nigra 'Guincho Purple' (black
    elder or bour tree) Deciduous shrub
Spiraea japonica 'Goldflame'
    Deciduous shrub

five more to try

Cytisus 'Lena' Deciduous shrub
Helenium 'Moerheim Beauty'
    Herbaceous perennial
Kirengeshoma palmata
    Herbaceous perennial
Magnolia × *soulangeana* Deciduous tree
Philadelphus 'Virginal' Deciduous shrub

a bit more exotic

Neillia thibetica Deciduous shrub

Plants for acid soil

A comparatively small number of plants enjoy a limefree soil, but those that do will just not succeed in an alkaline soil – most will die. They include some of our best-loved plants such as pieris, azaleas, rhododendrons, and most heathers. One way to grow lime haters in a garden that is not ideal is to form raised beds by building low walls or using railroad ties and filling them to a depth of 24 in (60 cm) with a limefree medium – usually sold as ericaceous medium.

top ten

Calluna vulgaris 'H. E. Beale' Evergreen shrub
Camellia x *williamsii* 'Anticipation' Evergreen shrub
Celmisia spectabilis (New Zealand daisy) Evergreen perennial
Daboecia cantabrica 'Bicolor' Evergreen shrub
Enkianthus cernuus rubens Deciduous shrub
Kalmia latifolia (calico bush) Evergreen shrub
Lithodora diffusa 'Heavenly Blue' Evergreen shrub
Meconopsis grandis (Himalayan blue poppy) Herbaceous perennial
Pieris 'Forest Flame' Evergreen shrub
Rhododendron 'Moerheim' Dwarf evergreen shrub

five more to try

Erica cinerea Evergreen shrub
Eucryphia x *nymansensis* Evergreen tree
Gentiana x *macaulayi* Semi-evergreen perennial
Magnolia liliiflora 'Nigra' Deciduous shrub
Phlox stolonifera Evergreen perennial

a bit more exotic

Clethra delavayi (sweet pepper bush) Deciduous shrub

Summer- flowering *Verbascum chaixii* 'Album.'

Plants for alkaline (limy) soils

Alkaline soils are ideal for a wide range of plants, whose roots seem to enjoy the free-draining, light, warm conditions. The addition of organic matter in the form of compost, rotted manure, and mulches will make the soil more water-retentive, and irrigation during dry periods will help the plants get established quickly. An excess of lime can cause a defficiency of other trace elements, locking them up in the soil and showing as a discoloration on the leaf. Iron and magnesium both show as yellowing of the leaf or chlorosis, caused by too limy a soil.

top ten

Campanula glomerata 'Superba' (clustered bell flower) Herbaceous perennial
Deutzia x *hybrida* 'Mont Rose' Deciduous shrub
Dianthus gratianopolitanus (cheddar pink) Evergreen perennial
Kolkwitzia amabilis 'Pink Cloud' (beauty bush) Deciduous shrub
Malus floribunda (Japanese crab apple) Deciduous tree
Philadelphus 'Belle Etoile' (mock orange) Deciduous shrub
Pulsatilla vulgaris (pasque flower) Herbaceous perennial
Sorbus aria 'Lutescens' (whitebeam) Deciduous tree
Syringa meyeri 'Palibin' (lilac) Deciduous shrub
Verbascum chaixii 'Album' (nettle-leaved mullein) Semi-evergreen perennial

five more to try

Buddlea davidii Deciduous shrub
Euphorbia myrsinites Evergreen perennial
Osmanthus delavayi Evergreen shrub
Santolina rosmarinifolia Evergreen shrub
Sarcococca hookeriana Evergreen shrub

a bit more exotic

Cercis siliquastrum (Judas tree) Deciduous tree

Plants for exposed sites

Cold biting wind can dry out the foliage of newly planted shrubs and trees before they are able to take up moisture and so kill the plant. It can also loosen plants in the ground. Tall young herbaceous plants need to be staked to prevent them from being blown over before they flower. Check staked plants in fall and spring to make sure stakes have not come loose and straps are not too tight. A temporary screen of burlap or net will protect new plants until they get established. For a more permanent form of shelter, plants themselves provide the best windbreak. They let the wind filter through the branches, whereas solid fences or walls force the wind to blow over the top and cause heavy turbulence on the side that is supposed to be sheltered.

top ten

Achillea filipendulina Evergreen perennial
Arbutus unedo (strawberry tree)
  Evergreen tree
Aster alpinus Herbaceous perennial

Betula pendula (silver birch) Deciduous tree

Crataegus monogyna (common hawthorn) Deciduous tree
Laburnum × *watereri* 'Vossii' (golden rain) Deciduous tree
Nepeta × *faassenii* (catmint) Herbaceous perennial
Sorbus aucuparia (rowan, mountain ash) Deciduous tree
Spiraea 'Arguta' (bridal wreath) Deciduous shrub
Ulex europaeus 'Flore Pleno' (gorse, whin, furze) Evergreen shrub

five more to try

Acer pseudoplatanus Deciduous tree
Euonymus europaeus 'Red Cascade' Deciduous shrub
Gaultheria shallon Evergreen shrub
Prunus spinosa (blackthorn, sloe) Deciduous tree
Rosa rugosa Deciduous shrub (zones 2-9)

a bit more exotic

Ledum groenlandicum (Labrador tea) Evergreen shrub

Spiraea **'Arguta' forms a dense bush.**

Plants with aromatic foliage

A great number of aromatic plants are natives of the Mediterranean, where they enjoy light, free-draining, stony soils that are low in nutrients and moisture, plus lots of sun. The addition of sharp sand and coarse grit will help to lighten heavy soils; choosing a site in full sun but sheltered from cold winds, frost, and heavy rain will reduce the risk of the plants dying in their first winter.

top ten

Caryopteris × *clandonensis* 'Kew Blue' Deciduous shrub
Lavandula angustifolia (English lavender) Evergreen shrub
Mentha suaveolens 'Variegata' Herbaceous perennial
Myrtus communis (common myrtle) Evergreen shrub
Perovskia 'Blue Spire' Deciduous sub-shrub
Rosmarinus officinalis (rosemary) Evergreen shrub
Ruta graveolens 'Jackman's Blue' (rue) Evergreen sub-shrub
Santolina chamaecyparissus Evergreen shrub
Skimmia × *confusa* 'Kew Green' Evergreen shrub
Thuja occidentalis (white cedar) Evergreen conifer

five more to try

Eucalyptus gunnii Evergreen tree
Illicium anisatum (Chinese arise) Evergreen shrub
Lavandula stoechas (French lavender) Evergreen shrub
Populus balsamifera Deciduous tree
Rosa eglanteria Deciduous shrub

a bit more exotic

Umbellularia californica (headache tree) Evergreen tree

Plants for seashore sites

There is no shortage of plants that can be grown in coastal areas, but as well as tolerating severe winds, they must be able to put up with salt deposits on their foliage. Many perennials will thrive at the seashore, though they may be susceptible to bad weather in spring when the new shoots are emerging. Shrubs may be cut back by severe spring weather, especially if they put on a late flush of soft growth the previous fall. But it usually acts as a form of natural clipping, and the plants soon recover and grow away quite happily. Evergreens are prone to leaf scorch on the seaward side of the plant, when salt-laden winds burn the foliage; conifers are particuarly vulnerable.

top ten

Anthemis punctata subsp. *cupaniana* Herbaceous perennial
Artemisia arborescens (wormwood) Evergreen shrub
Centranthus ruber (red valerian) Herbaceous perennial

Escallonia rubra var. *macrantha* Evergreen shrub
Fascicularia bicolor subsp. *bicolor* Terrestrial bromeliad
Fuchsia magellanica Deciduous shrub
Hippophae rhamnoides (sea buckthorn) Deciduous tree
Olearia macrodonta Evergreen shrub
Othonna cheirifolia Evergreen shrub
Tamarix ramosissima (tamarisk) Deciduous shrub

five more to try

Buddleia globosa Deciduous shrub
Elaeagnus pungens 'Maculata' Evergreen shrub
Eryngium × *oliverianum* Herbaceous perennial
Lupinus arboreus (tree lupine) Evergreen shrub
Populus alba (poplar) Deciduous tree

a bit more exotic

Escallonia 'Iveyi' Evergreen shrub

Red-flowered *Centranthus ruber* enjoys a maritime site and spreads over a wide area.

Plants for cut flowers

Not all species last well in water. The plants listed here make ideal cut flowers. If you want lots of flowers, you can plant a cutting bed of annuals and perennials. Make the bed in a sheltered site and support plants to prevent wind damage. The soil should be moisture retentive but not too rich: excessive nitrogenous fertilizer encourage leaf growth instead of flowers.

top ten

Achillea 'Coronation Gold' (yarrow) Evergreen perennial
Astilbe × *arendsii* 'Fanal' Deciduous perennial
Callistephus chinensis 'Ostrich Plume' (China aster) Annual
Camellia × *williamsii* 'Anticipation' Evergreen shrub
Chrysanthemum Herbaceous perennial
Delphinium 'Butterball' Herbaceous perennial
Forsythia × *intermedia* 'Karl Sax' Deciduous shrub
Geum 'Mrs J. Bradshaw' Herbaceous perennial
Paeonia lactiflora 'Bowl of Beauty' Herbaceous perennial
Rosa Deciduous shrub
Zantedeschia aethiopica (arum lily) Herbaceous perennial

five more to try

Freesia Perennial grown from corms
Kniphofia 'Wrexham Buttercup' Herbaceous perennial
Rhododendron decorum Evergreen shrub
Rudbeckia fulgida Herbaceous perennial
Tulipa 'Fringed Elegance' Bulb Annual

a bit more exotic

Yucca gloriosa Evergreen shrub

A sheltered garden allows tender protea (on the left) to grow and prevents the flower heads of the white agapanthus from being damaged by wind.

Plants for sheltered gardens

I haven't met a gardener who hasn't wished for a part of his garden to be different from whatever nature has provided, and I am as bad as the rest. Like most northern-hemisphere gardeners, I would love to be able to grow outside all those tender plants that exist only in heated conservatories in my part of the world. Wishful thinking, I know, but there is a range of plants that, given the most favored spot in the garden, will survive and even thrive. Then, if you wish, you really can be one up on your gardening friends. But don't brag too much: sooner or later, a freak frost or prolonged period of wet or dry weather will kill your treasures.

Walls facing the afternoon sun and sheltered from cold winds will suit a lot of delicate plants.

Lightening the soil by the addition of grit and using a mulch of white gravel to reflect the light will all help. Providing overhead shelter from the worst of winter rain will do much to prevent tender plants from becoming waterlogged. Small plants may be protected by covering them with a sheet of glass raised on bricks. Cover larger plants with clear plastic stretched over a framework of bamboo stakes, like a wigwam.

———————————•———————————

top ten

Echium wildpretii Herbaceous perennial
Fremontodendron mexicanum Evergreen shrub
Hedychium densiflorum (ginger lily) Herbaceous perennial
Lapageria rosea (Chilean bellflower) Evergreen climber
Myosotidium hortensia (Chatham Island forget-me-not) Evergreen perennial
Paeonia cambessedesii Herbaceous perennial
Paulownia tomentosa (foxglove tree) Deciduous tree
Pittosporum tobira (Japanese mock orange) Evergreen tree
Protea cynaroides (king protea) Evergreen shrub
Trachelospermum jasminoides (star jasmine) Evergreen climber

five more to try

Acacia dealbata Evergreen shrub
Allium cristophii Bulb
Dianthus alpinus 'Joan's Blood' Herbaceous perennial
Disanthus cercidifolius Deciduous shrub
Sophora davidii Deciduous shrub

a bit more exotic

Pseudopanax ferox Evergreen tree

Actinidia kolmikta **produces fragrant white flowers in summer, but is grown primarily for its stunning foliage.**

Plants for walls

One of the biggest problems with growing plants up a wall is that the soil conditions at the base of the wall can be totally unsuitable. The area is usually contaminated with builders' rubble, and if the wall is part of the house, the rain doesn't wet the soil because of the roof overhang. Any available moisture is absorbed by the porous wall and concrete foundation before plants can take it up, and it will be necessary to water regularly and enrich the soil with compost. Some plants can be positioned with their roots 12 in (30 cm) away from the wall and then trained toward it.

From an aesthetic point of view, consider the color of the wall. White or cream flowers will be lost against a white-plastered surface, as will red-flowering climbers on red brick. In the northern hemisphere, east-facing walls are not suitable for spring-flowering plants, because the morning sun after a frost can scorch buds. South-facing walls can be very hot and are good for growing and training a fruiting peach tree on. West-facing walls get the evening sun and are ideal for most plants, especially those that need pampering. North-facing walls are sunless and cold, but there are still plenty of plants that will succeed and flower there. In the southern hemisphere, north-facing is sunny and south-facing likely to be cheerless.

The automatic choice of plant for a wall is a climber, but there are many excellent free-standing shrubs that, without support, will hug a wall.

top ten

Camellia sasanqua 'Narumigata' Evergreen shrub, sunny wall

Ceanothus 'Puget Blue' Evergreen shrub, sunny wall

Chaenomeles speciosa 'Moerloosei' (flowering quince) Deciduous shrub, sunny wall

Cytisus battandieri (pineapple broom) Semi-evergreen shrub, sunny wall

Euonymus fortunei 'Silver Queen' Evergreen shrub, sunny or shaded wall

Exochorda x *macrantha* 'The Bride' (pearl bush) Deciduous shrub, sunny or shaded wall

Hedera canariensis 'Gloire de Marengo' (Canary Island ivy) Evergreen climber, sunny or shaded wall

Hydrangea anomala subsp. *petiolaris* (climbing hydrangea) Deciduous climber, shaded wall

Lonicera sempervirens (trumpet honeysuckle) Evergreen shrub, shaded wall

Parthenocissus henryana (Virginia creeper) Deciduous climber, sunny or shaded wall.

five more to try

Actinidia kolomikta Deciduous climber, sunny wall

Akebia quinata Evergreen climber, sunny wall

Clematis armandii Evergreen climber, sunny wall

Clianthus puniceus 'Albus' Evergreen climber, sunny wall

Jasminum officinale f. *affine* Deciduous climber, sunny wall

a bit more exotic

Mandevilla laxa (Chilean jasmine) Deciduous climber, sunny wall

Plants for barrier planting

The first line of defense for most gardens is the boundary. It is so much nicer and more natural in most locations to use living plants for the perimeter to form a hedge or boundary planting. The screen may be necessary for privacy or shelter or even security, and deciduous or evergreen plants or a mixture of both can be used. Plants allow the wind to filter through rather than blowing over the top and causing turbulence on the garden side. At the same time, the leaves and branches filter out traffic noise. Hedges can be formal or informal, depending on how they are clipped (see page 92 for more information).

For a long-term planting such as a hedge, the site should be well prepared with lots of compost and old farmyard manure added to the bottom of the planting trench. Incorporate some slow-acting fertilizer, such as bonemeal, into the soil as you fill it back in. Choose a site that is weed free, especially of perennial weeds. If they are allowed to become established among hedging plants, they will be difficult to remove and use the hedge as a secure base camp from which to spread at will. Clipping or pruning when plants are young will thicken up the hedge at the base, with less risk of gaps occuring low down in the hedge.

———————————— • ————————————

top ten
Alnus cordata (Italian alder) Deciduous tree
Berberis x *stenophylla* Evergreen shrub
Cotoneaster lacteus Evergreen shrub
x *Cupressocyparis leylandii* 'Castlewellan' (Golden leyland) Evergreen conifer
Elaeagnus x *ebbingei* 'Limelight' Evergreen shrub

Griselinia littoralis Evergreen shrub
Ilex aquifolium (common holly) Evergreen shrub or tree
Prunus laurocerasus (laurel, cherry laurel) Evergreen shrub
Taxus baccata (yew) Evergreen conifer
Thuja plicata (western red cedar) Evergreen conifer

five more to try
Chamaecyparis lawsoniana Evergreen conifer
Escallonia 'Pride of Donard' Evergreen shrub
Fagus sylvatica Deciduous tree
Pittosporum tenuifolium Evergreen tree
Viburnum tinus Evergreen shrub

a bit more exotic
Chaenomeles speciosa Deciduous shrub

Viburnum tinus is evergreen and flowers in winter, bringing welcome cheer to the garden. A deciduous viburnum, V. x carlcephalum, is worth growing for its red fall foliage.

Plants for fall leaf color

There are few sights more spectacular than autumn sunlight on a mature Japanese maple, its rich canopy a blaze of red. Yet it needs only one gale or night's frost to bring the display to an end with the leaves scattered to the four corners. If you are planting for fall color, choose a sheltered site where the wind can't remove the leaves prematurely. Avoid extremes of dry and wet ground, and areas in deep shade. A feed in early summer will encourage the plant to make new shoots and even more leaves that will change color. It's not only deciduous trees that change color in the fall: some garden conifers do, too, such as *Thuja orientalis* 'Rosedalis,' which has bright yellow foliage in spring, gray-green in summer, and plum-purple in late fall.

———————————•———————————

top ten

Acer palmatum 'Chitoseyama' (Japanese maple) Deciduous tree
Amelanchier lamarckii (snowy mespilus) Deciduous shrub or tree
Cercidiphyllum japonicum (Katsura tree) Deciduous tree
Cotinus 'Grace' (smoke bush) Deciduous shrub
Euonymus alatus (winged spindle) Deciduous shrub
Fothergilla major Deciduous shrub
Liquidambar styraciflua (sweet gum) Deciduous tree
Parrotia persica (Persian ironwood) Deciduous tree
Prunus sargentii Deciduous tree
Rhus typhina 'Dissecta' (stag's horn sumac) Deciduous shrub

five more to try

Carya ovata (hickory) Deciduous tree
Malus tschonoskii (crab apple) Deciduous tree
Nandina domestica 'Fire Power' (heavenly bamboo) Deciduous shrub
Quercus rubra (red oak) Deciduous tree
Sorbus sargentiana (rowan) Deciduous tree

a bit more exotic

Nyssa sinensis (Chinese tupelo) Deciduous tree

Rowan (*Sorbus*) and cherry (*Prunus*) in brilliant shades of autumn color contrast with the variegated holly (*Ilex*).

Poppies will self-seed to reappear next year.

Plants for the wild garden

Like any other part of the garden, the wild garden has to be managed. If not, it ceases to be wild, becoming instead an overgrown, weed-infested piece of ground. It is worth remembering that many wild flowers are, in fact, fully qualified weeds, and while buttercup, ragweed, bindweed, and willow herb all have pretty flowers, they are awful weeds to let loose in the garden. They are quick to spread and very difficult to control. Luckily, there are lots of wild plants that are harmless in the garden and add greatly to the overall display while requiring minimum attention. They are happy to grow in impoverished soil in woodland or open ground, provided they are not smothered by more aggressive plants.

top ten

Aquilegia vulgaris (Granny's bonnet) Herbaceous perennial
Centaurea cyanus (bachelor's buttons) Annual
Corylus avellana (hazel) Deciduous shrub
Digitalis purpurea (foxglove) Biennial or short-lived perennial
Geranium pratense (meadow cranesbill) Herbaceous perennial
Hyacinthoides non-scripta (English bluebell) Bulbous perennial
Leucanthemum vulgare (ox-eye daisy) Herbaceous perennial
Papaver rhoeas (corn poppy, Flanders poppy) Annual
Primula vulgaris (primrose) Evergreen perennial
Rosa rubignosa (sweet briar) Deciduous shrub

five more to try

Alchemilla alpina (alpine lady's mantle) Herbaceous perennial
Arum maculatum (lords and ladies) Tuberous perennial
Gentiana verna (spring gentian) Evergreen perennial
Iris pseudacorus (yellow flag) Evergreen rhizomatous perennial
Pulsatilla vulgaris (pasque flower) Herbaceous perennial

a bit more exotic

Dactylorhiza fuchsii (common spotted orchid) Deciduous perennial

Snake's head fritillary (*Fritillaria meleagris*) (zones 3-8) naturalized in the meadow at Magdalen College, Oxford, England. Fritillaries are ideal scattered through an area of grass that can be left uncut, but will not survive in a lawn that is mowed regularly.

take any two plants

Cheese and wine, peaches and cream – they just seem to go together, and so it is with some groups of plants. Allowing for height, climate, and soil type, the plants almost seem to grow better together and bring out the best in their companions, fitting into the garden plan as an area of planting that will be noticed and copied.

roses and dwarf bulbs

Roses are one of our all-time favorites. Bush roses are colorful, repeat flowering, many are fragrant, and they are available in a broad range of colors. The trouble is that they make a display only from early summer to mid fall. The rest of the year they are frankly dead looking. Lots of plant combinations have been tried to cheer them up, including heathers and ground coverers such as ajuga and vinca, but none is really satisfactory because they all climb partway up the stems. The best method I have found is to use dwarf bulbs. By planting spring- and fall-flowering crocus, dwarf tulips, and snowdrops, the bed of roses will be in color for most of the year. The foliage of dwarf bulbs dies away quickly, or if you prefer, the bulbs can be lifted after flowering and stored for replanting the following season.

The site should be out in the open, not shaded, and on a good loam or clay soil. Dig in lots of compost and farmyard manure, and cultivate deeply to loosen the soil and give the roots a good start.

Bush roses are budded onto a rootstock, and the union between the two must not be buried too deeply, as this encourages suckers to grow from the rootstock. If they are not removed quickly and as close to the stem or root as possible, they will grow faster than the variety and eventually take over.

Rosa 'Pot o' Gold' forms a neater bush than many roses, but it is still not very interesting in spring. An underplanting of bulbs will make the bed more cheerful.

Do's and don'ts

• Don't mix colors and varieties of roses in a small bed; one mass of color will look better.

• Don't plant new roses in a bed where roses have already been grown: they will suffer from rose sickness.

• Don't allow suckers (shoots) to grow from the rose rootstock.

• Do choose scented rose varieties, such as 'Fragrant Cloud' or 'Irish Eyes.'

• Do feed regularly in summer with rose fertilizer.

• Don't plant bulbs too close to the roses.

• Do plant a good quantity of each variety of bulb — groups of 30-50 are ideal.

Dig a planting hole larger than the grafted spread of the roots and add a handful of bonemeal to the hole around the roots of each rose. Bush roses should be planted 24 in (60 cm) apart. After firming the soil around the roots, shorten the shoots to 4–6 in (10–15 cm) and remove any weak or damaged stems.

Roses require routine maintenance: remove the dead flowers and feed them throughout the summer. Cut the plants back in early winter, removing about half of the shoots. Do the main pruning in early spring, cutting back shoots to 8-12 in (20-30 cm) from the ground and removing any weak and diseased stems.

In order that they remain good friends, it is essential that the bulbs don't compete with the roses. Plant dwarf varieties of bulbs that flower when the roses are dormant. These don't have an excess of foliage and are quick to die down, leaving the roses center stage for the summer. Bulbs of crocus, snowdrop, tulip, scilla, anemone, aconite, and miniature iris will all add color to the bed, and for the fall, plant hardy cyclamen.

shrubs and herbaceous plants

Herbaceous beds are back in fashion, but they still suffer from the problem that made them unpopular years ago – the fact that they can look dead and uninteresting in winter. Most perennials die down in late fall, leaving a few evergreens that flower in winter such as hellebores to keep the bed looking alive. Bulbs can help to fill the gap, but since herbaceous plants have to be lifted and divided every few years, there is a risk of disturbing the bulbs.

Mixing some shrubs into the bed is the best way to add color and plant and leaf shape to brighten the winter show. Choose evergreen shrubs, especially those that have variegated foliage to boost the off-season display. Try to design in shrubs that won't get too large; otherwise, they tend to swamp the bed and hide the main summer display of perennials. A few winter-flowering deciduous shrubs can be included, such as *Daphne mezereum* – its compact shape and superb perfume more than compensate for the lack of leaves.

The herbaceous bed is prone to weeds, and if they invade a clump of plants, it is usually best to dump the clump rather than trying to remove the weeds. It is essential that you start with a bed free of perennial weeds and that you are careful not to import weeds with clumps of free plants given to you by "friends."

Shades of green and gold provided by conifers, hostas, and euonymus, with a splash of blue ceanothus.

Do's and don'ts

• Don't plant all the shrubs at one end of the bed: mix them throughout.

• Don't plant tall-growing shrubs that will swamp the other plants.

• Don't use summer-flowering shrubs: their effect will be lost when the herbaceous plants in the bed are looking at their best.

• Do divide the herbaceous perennials every three years.

• Do keep a close eye out for slugs and snails; they love tender young shoots.

• Do plant shrubs to extend the flowering season to fall and spring as well as winter.

• Do cut the herbaceous perennials back in the fall to help clear up the bed.

A colorful display of bulbs naturalized in grass. The foliage of the narcissus will last a lot longer than that of the *Anemone blanda*, so mowing will have to be delayed until it has died down.

lawns and bulbs

With a bit of thought, this can be the best garden combination of all. Lawns can be boringly green (or yellow) and require a lot of maintenance to keep them in a presentable state. I once heard a lawn described as a collective term for a lot of weeds. It can become strikingly beautiful if dwarf bulbs are naturalized through it and allowed to multiply each year, forming drifts of color. The level of maintenance is not increased as the dying foliage is removed with the grass. The trick is to avoid tall-growing bulbs with large leaves, such as daffodils, and those that flower in late spring, long after grass cutting has started.

A new lawn sown or laid as sod in the fall is ideal, since this is the best time to plant bulbs. Plant them just before the seed is sown or the sod laid, and they will grow through the grass. A dense planting will look more impressive and be more memorable than a scattering of flowers dotted all over the lawn.

Established lawns require a bit more work. The sod needs to be lifted, the bulbs spread on the soil, and the sod replaced. Or individual holes can be made in the grass, a bulb placed in each hole and infilled with fine soil.

Do's and don'ts

• Don't apply weedkillers to the lawn until all bulb foliage has died down and the bulbs are dormant.

• Don't cut the grass until the bulb foliage has died away – usually about six weeks after flowering.

• Do give the grass a cut in late fall before the bulbs start to grow, to keep it short at flowering time.

• Don't use summer-flowering bulbs in the lawn, for obvious reasons.

• Do feed the bulbs immediately after flowering and before the foliage dies down.

• Do plant the bulbs at a depth of two to three times the height of the bulb.

Dwarf narcissus, crocus, and snowdrops make a wonderful show in the spring. Where an area of grass can be allowed to remain uncut for a longer period, bluebells, fritillaries, and wild orchids may be encouraged. In the fall, *Cyclamen hederifolium* (zones 5-9) followed by *Cyclamen coum* will make a brave show in short grass.

trees and ground cover

Deciduous trees add height and shape to a garden and provide interest all year round – even in winter, the bare, twiggy tracery of branches adds to the overall picture. There are trees to suit even the very smallest of gardens, but they can be difficult to underplant. All trees cast a shadow, and if the garden is well endowed with different trees, the amount of shade can be considerable. Tree roots spread far and wide in search of water and nutrients, and as a result, the ground directly under the canopy of the tree is dry, riddled with roots, impoverished, and in shade. Any rain that does penetrate in summer when the tree is in leaf falls as large drops that have collected on the leaves, which can damage small plants or wash away soil.

Do's and don'ts

• **Don't** try to cultivate the soil under the trees; you will damage the roots. Instead form planting holes between the roots and carefully insert small container-grown plants.

• **Don't** use long stakes to support the newly planted trees. Short stakes allow the tree to build up a better root system (see also Staking, Training, and Tying, page 40).

• **Don't** try to establish ground-cover plants in soil that has a perennial weed problem. Deal with it first.

• **Don't** let the plants go short of water during the first season until the roots are established.

• **Do** plant the trees at the right spacing to prevent them from growing into their neighbors.

• **Do** remove the bulk of the leaves that fall in autumn, as they will smother the smaller ground coverers.

• **Do** use plants that will spread to cover all the bare ground such as bugle (*Ajuga*), pachysandra, and periwinkle (*Vinca*).

• **Do** plant some evergreen shrubs as a contrast to deciduous trees – *Sarcococca*, the sweetly scented Christmas box, is ideal.

Unless your garden is 1,000 sq yd in size, avoid planting large forest trees such as oak, beech, and ash. Instead, go for the garden forms of the mountain ash (*Sorbus*), flowering cherry (*Prunus*), false acacia (*Robinia*), and crab apples (*Malus*). It is usual to buy garden trees as standards, grown on a clear stem or trunk with no side branches below 6 ft (2 m) or as half standards, with a bare trunk 3 ft (1 m) high. To make best use of the space and to cover the soil, underplant the trees with plants that can survive in shady, dry, root-infested ground .

As their name suggests, ground-cover plants are plants that cover the soil. While many of them are low growing, others are of reasonable height with dense foliage that prevents weeds from growing below them. Species that can tolerate conditions under the trees include *Geranium macrorrhizum, Lamium maculatum,* and the fern *Polypodium vulgare.* They form a lower level of interest while covering the soil and reducing weeding. With a little planning, it is possible to have year-round color by incorporating some bulbs such as winter aconites, hardy cyclamen, and *Anemone blanda* (zones 4-8), which will naturalize, spreading through the other plants.

The white-barked birch (*Betula utilis* var. jacquemontii) underplanted with the bugle plant (*Ajuga reptans*) (zones 3-9) and foxgloves (*Digitalis*).

If rabbits or other digging mammals are a problem in your garden, enclose the area with a fence to keep them out. To stop them from burrowing under the fence, bury some netting below it and put net across the gate as well.

Growing vegetables from seed

There is something very satisfying about sowing vegetables, watching them grow, looking after them, and then harvesting them and enjoying that homegrown flavor.

Except in very small gardens where space is at a premium, the majority of vegetables should be sown in a seed bed and remain there until they are harvested or transplanted. In either case, it is important that the bed is well prepared, and there is no point in starting to cultivate until the soil is workable. In winter, the area should be covered with a 6 in (15 cm) layer of rotted farmyard manure, then dug over and left rough for the frost to break down. By spring the lumps are easily worked with a rake or a fork, to leave a fairly fine tilth with no lumps or large stones. Don't cultivate too deeply; the seed bed needs to be firm but not packed down. Scatter a general-purpose fertilizer at 2 oz (60 g) per sq yd and rake it into the top 3 in (8 cm). A final rake-over to level the site and remove any debris, and you are ready for sowing.

Tips

• Birds cause enormous damage to fruit crops, and pigeons are fond of green vegetables, removing the leaves faster than they can grow. Fine-mesh plastic nets on a wooden or metal structure 6 ft (2 m) high and covering 12ft x 15ft (20 sq m) should protect most crops, provided the nets don't become damaged and let birds enter.

• On light, sandy soils, growing a hedge of lavender around the kitchen garden will look attractive, and the aromatic foliage will disguise the smell of carrot leaves and foil the deadly carrot fly, which is attracted by their scent. It lays its eggs beside the young carrot, and the resulting grub tunnels into the root and destroys it. Another method is to make a 12 in (30 cm) high screen of horticultural fleece around the bed of carrots to keep the low-flying insects out.

Soft and bush fruit

Fruit is very much a part of the kitchen garden, and picking summer fruit can be memorable. Strawberries and raspberries often disappear from the basket before they get to the kitchen door. Black, red, and white currants all make traditional desserts, as do gooseberries, blackberries, and loganberries.

Aim to buy certified stock of fruit that has been declared free from a whole range of diseases that cause a reduction in yield and stunt the plants. Most soft fruits like a sunny site sheltered from cold winds and a soil that has been enriched with lots of compost and old farmyard manure. Space rows well apart so the bushes are not shading each other. Raspberry canes can grow to 6 ft (2 m) high: keep them on the north side of the plot to avoid casting shade. If there is more than one line of canes, the rows should be 6 ft (2 m) apart for the same reason.

Growing raspberries

Raspberries are supported on wires running the length of the row. You need two wires attached to wooden posts and strung 24 in (60 cm) and 60 in (150 cm) above the ground respectively. The fruiting stems of the raspberry must be tied to the wires 4 in (10 cm) apart. When pruning, any tall shoots should be cut back to 6 ft (1.8 m) and surplus stems removed at ground level. This makes it easier to pick the fruit. After fruiting, those stems are cut off as close to the ground as possible and are replaced by that year's new shoots.

Growing strawberries

Strawberries should be grown in weedfree soil and can be planted on level ground. But if the earth is wet, the plants can be set on ridges of soil 3 ft (1 m) apart. Space the plants 18 in (45 cm) apart in the rows. The strawberry plants should be planted at the same depth as they were when potted up. The earlier they can be planted in the fall, when the soil is still warm, the larger the crop will be the following summer.

It is amazing how much produce can be grown in a small area and still leave space for sweet peas.

mediterranean garden

It may not be possible to have a Mediterranean-style area in your garden – you need a site in full sun, and if the ground slopes, it should face the sun. To me, a Mediterranean garden conjures up images of hot gravel and stones, heavy dry heat, the sound of insects, terracotta-painted walls, shady seats, figs, vines, and plumbago growing up the walls, plus a mixture of aromatic smells.

The chosen spot has to be the most favored in the garden, sheltered from the wind and cold frosts in the spring. Most Mediterranean plants hate to have wet feet, so the soil will need to be free draining, with lots of added grit to keep it loose, open, and easily warmed by the sun. Surface the beds with a layer of gravel, which will warm up quickly, hold the heat, and act as a mulch to reduce weeding. On heavy clay soils, it just won't work – the soil dries out and forms surface cracks during hot periods, causing roots to suffer and water to drain away below the root zone. Instead, create a planting area by building walls of planks or ornamental bricks and filling the raised bed with imported sandy soil to keep the plant roots well above the clay.

Plants that are not totally hardy can be grown in terracotta pots and moved to a frostproof glasshouse or conservatory before winter sets in. If your budget will only run to plain plastic pots, plunge them them into the bed up to the rim and rake the gravel back over. They can be lifted and cleaned off ready for frostfree winter storage. Deciduous plants that start to grow early in the year and are prone to damage but not killed by frost, can be protected by covering the plant with chopped-up bracken, straw, or coarse bark mulch. Remove it after all risk of frost is over in late spring.

> ## Great plants for Mediterranean-style gardens
> **Berberis empetrifolia** Evergreen shrub
> **Carpenteria californica** Evergreen shrub
> **Fabiana imbricata f. violacea** Evergreen shrub.
> **Hibiscus syriacus** 'Oiseau Bleu' Deciduous shrub
> **Lavandula angustifolia** (English lavender) Evergreen aromatic shrub
> **Lavandula stoechas** (French lavender) Evergreen aromatic shrub
> **Yucca gloriosa 'Variegata'** (Spanish dagger) Evergreen perennial
> Don't forget all the edibles for warm, sunny walls: figs, vines, cherries, and peaches. Then there are the herbs that, if grown in a hot, dry soil, will have a much enhanced flavor – sage and thyme, for example.

> ## Tip
> Soft shoots produced late in the season are more prone to damage from frost than shoots that are well hardened. In early fall, give all the plants in the Mediterranean garden a liquid feed high in potash but with no nitrogen fertilizer. The potash will harden up the young growths, and omitting nitrogen won't prompt the plant into fresh growth.

Left: **If you can grow oranges, you can have a Mediterranean-type garden. This is the real thing, in Mallorca, Spain. In more temperate climates the citrus trees (1) would need to be grown in containers and moved to shelter in winter. Cyclamen (2) will survive outside only in frostfree areas.**
Right: **Spiky-leaved architectural plants and tiled paths give a hot Mediterranean feel to this New Zealand garden.**

cottage garden

Original cottage gardens were the result of random planting of bits and pieces given by friends and cuttings taken from the "big house." There was seldom any overall design, and if a plant proved through time to be too large, it was simply moved to another position. Space was at a premium, most of the ground being used for growing essential food crops, so the less useful but more decorative plants filled the gaps and covered walls and fences.

When I imagine a cottage garden, I think of brick or gravel surfaced paths edged with stones or bricks and plants tumbling over. A mass of bright and muted colors splash over the ground, and plants of every shape and size mixed at random. Above all, I can almost take hold of the jumble of scents that evoke childhood memories.

As an area within a larger plot, the cottage garden doesn't have to be particularly big. You can give it its own boundary by surrounding it with a low fence. Use rustic peeled bark trellis or an old-fashioned picket fence, and grow perennials such as hollyhocks (*Alcea rosea*) and delphiniums or scrambling climbers such as clematis, roses, and honeysuckle (*Lonicera*) up and over the fence. The area can be in full sun or light shade, where foxgloves (*Digitalis*), poppies (*Papaver*), monkshood (*Aconitum*), columbine (*Aquilegia*), and evening primrose (*Oenothera*) will soon spread by seed.

Preparing the ground
Take your time preparing the soil and eliminate as many weeds as possible before planting. Heavy wet soils may need to be drained or opened up by digging a 2 in (5 cm) layer of coarse washed grit into the top 10 in (25 cm) of soil. Cottage gardens were never short of old farmyard manure, it was the one thing that there was plenty of, and it took the place of compost and fertilizer. Today it is not so readily available, and if you can't get hold of any, dig in as much compost as possible and apply 1 oz (30 g) of slow-release bonemeal per sq yd to the roots at planting time.

A small rustic alcove complete with wooden seat provides somewhere to sit in relaxing surroundings and enjoy the sun among the scent of honeysuckle, lavender, and pinks (*Dianthus*).

> **Tip**
>
> Any gaps can be filled in summer by sowing seed of annuals such as nasturtium (*Tropaeolum*) and bachelor's buttons (*Centaurea cyanus*) directly into the spaces, thinning them out as necessary.

The mixture of perennials and lack of order combine to give a cottagey feel.

> **Great plants for cottage gardens**
>
> *Alcea rosea* **'Chater's Double'** (hollyhock) Biennial
> *Lathyrus latifolius* (everlasting pea) Perennial
> *Lathyrus odoratus* (sweet pea) Annual
> *Philadelphus* **'Belle Etoile'** (bride's blossom) Shrub
> *Rosmarinus officinalis* (rosemary) Shrub
> *Tropaeolum* **Gleam Series** (nasturtium) Annual

bog garden

If you have an area in the garden that is permanently wet or waterlogged and it is either too expensive to drain or there is no suitable outlet to take the water away, then turn the problem to your advantage and convert the area into a bog garden. The first thing to find out is whether the soil remains wet all year round, or if it is only a problem in winter or after prolonged rainfall. To succeed as a bog garden, the site needs to be constantly wet – plants that like those conditions won't survive if the soil dries out for a lengthy period. On the other hand, soil that is so waterlogged that it becomes stagnant and starts to smell won't support many plants, and the area will attract mosquitoes. If there is too much surface water, one option is to raise the soil level, allowing the plant roots to be in the wet while the crown of the plant is above the water.

Candelabra primulas, astilbe, and irises all enjoy having their feet in a moist soil.

Tip
When creating a bog garden, add a layer of wet rotted manure or leaf mold in the base of the hole, on top of the liner, to help retain moisture. Don't use peat – if it is allowed to dry out, it is practically impossible to re-wet.

Stepping stones through the planted areas will keep your footwear clean and at the same time let you see the plants growing in their own habitat. The area can be in sun or shade; there are plants that thrive in either.

Faking it Even if there is no suitably wet part in your garden, you can still have a bog area. Construct one by digging out a hole about 12 in (30 cm) deep and lining it with plastic sheeting, with a few holes pierced in the sides and base. Mix the excavated soil with an equal amount of moisture-retaining compost and replace the soil. The plastic retains the water, keeping the soil in the pit wet, yet it will drain slowly to prevent the soil from becoming saturated. Don't try to make a bog garden on sandy and gravel types of soil. They do not retain moisture. Bog gardens are often constructed beside a garden pond, and the overflow is directed into the bog, helping to keep the soil constantly wet. When it becomes

necessary to feed the plants, usually in late spring, use a high potash feed and water it in. If your bog garden is close to the pond, don't let the fertilizer drift into the open water.

Five great plants for wet areas
Astilbe Many varieties. Perennial
Clethra alnifolia (sweet pepper bush) Shrub
Hosta Many varieties. Perennial
Primula florindae (giant cowslip) Perennial
Rheum palmatum 'Atrosanguineum' (ornamental rhubarb) Perennial

woodland garden

A woodland garden cannot be arrived at overnight unless you have bought a wood, but if the planting is done carefully with the right species of plants, it is surprising how quickly it can come into being. The area of trees need not be massive – indeed, a woodland effect can be created in the corner of a medium-sized garden. A sheltered site will allow the young trees to grow quickly to form cover, although in many instances the main reason for planting trees is so that they will provide the initial shelter for the rest of the plants in the garden; it is only later that their value as a grove or wood becomes apparent. Try to choose a site that will get the sun at some part of the day; then, when the trees grow up, rays of sunlight can be encouraged to shine through into little glades, lighting up a chosen specimen in the surrounding gloom.

Dappled shade is enjoyed by primulas, hostas, rodgersia, irises, and rhododendrons.

Five great woodland trees

Betula pendula (silver birch) Deciduous
Fagus sylvatica (beech) Deciduous
Pinus nigra (Austrian pine) Evergreen conifer
Quercus rubra (red oak) Deciduous
Sorbus acuparia (rowan, mountain ash) Deciduous

Most soils will be satisfactory for woodland plants, provided there is enough depth for a good root run. Avoid thin soils overlying rock or chalk that is close to the surface, because the trees will become stunted and may die during a dry summer.

Pathways can be allowed to meander through the wood and cross over the existing tracks, giving the impression of a much larger area. They can be surfaced with chipped or peeled bark and edged with cut branches or logs.

A mixture of trees will produce a more interesting woodland, with lots of colors and leaf shapes. Mixing evergreens such as pine, holly, and spruce with deciduous species such as beech, oak, rowan, and ash will provide interest all year round and support a diverse range of wildlife.

If you are not in a hurry, plant young sapling trees called whips. Larger trees not only cost a lot more, but are slower to become established, and a percentage may die as a result of transplanting. Planting 6 ft (2 m) apart will allow the trees to form cover quickly and encourage them to grow with straight trunks. If the wood becomes too dense, thin it by removing the worst-shaped specimens and the least interesting varieties.

Tip

In the early years, fence the woodland area with rabbit-proof fencing to prevent these creatures from eating the young tree bark, which will stunt or kill the plant. Make very sure you fence the rabbits out and that there are none hiding in the long grass inside the wood when the fence is erected, or all your efforts will be wasted.

During the first few years, keep grass and weeds in the vicinity under control to prevent your plants from getting choked. This is best achieved by applying weedkiller or placing a 24 in (60 cm) collar

Woodland shade is ideal for ferns, elephant's ears (*Bergenia*), hostas, and Solomon's seal (*Polygonatum*). All form useful ground cover beneath the canopy of trees.

Five ground coverers

Cyclamen coum
Daphne laureola (spurge laurel)
Pachysandra terminalis (Japanese spurge)
Sarcococca humilis (Christmas box)
Vinca minor (periwinkle)

of old carpet around the base of each plant, making sure to water them regularly, since the collar will run the rain off.

As the trees grow, they will form a canopy, cutting out light and preventing weeds from growing. Autumn leaf fall will mean that after a few years a layer of leaf mold will build up and act as a mulch. Shade-loving ground-covering plants can be planted as an underskirt to provide you with one of the most interesting parts of the garden.

wildflower garden

Wild gardens can be very beautiful, but contrary to their name, they can be slow to mature and are not easy to manage. But if your garden is large, a wild garden is a great way to use part of the space.

Wild gardens I like, but there is a thin line between what I like and what I thoroughly dislike. There are wild gardens, and there are neglected, overgrown, and weed-infested gardens.

In winter a wild garden can look unkempt, with long grass and little color. For this reason, it should be tucked into a spot not too obvious from the house. It is the sort of area that you should come upon when out for a garden walk, or deliberately visit when it is in season and looking its best or stroll through on your way to another part of the garden. It can be in full sun or partial shade; a sloping site is acceptable, since the grass doesn't need to be mown too frequently. Even a small corner will accommodate a lot of different plants and will soon become a haven for a range of interesting wildlife.

Soil type   Any soil type will do, but if you can avoid the extremes of acidic and alkaline, you will be able to accommodate a larger range of plants. Most wildflowers prefer an impoverished soil. They dislike ground that has been enriched with fertilizer, which will encourage growth at the expense of flowers and, in many cases, even kill the plants or cause them to suffer from competition from other plants. Some gardeners are fortunate enough to have a deep loam soil: if you are one of the lucky ones, remove most of the soil from the wild garden area and reuse it where it will be appreciated, just leaving a thin layer over

the subsoil. There are wild plant species for all types of soil, but heavy wet soils are more difficult to work with.

Keeping the garden going   Germination of the seed of annual wildflowers can be hit or miss. Some types of plant have a greater chance of success than others, and quite often by the start of the third season, some of the original species will have died out. Young seedlings can be suffocated by strong-growing grass and other weeds.

Rather than relying on nature, you can harvest about half of the seed by cutting off the seed heads and shaking them over a sheet of paper. Pour seed into paper bags and store it in a cool dry place over winter. Sow some of it in the wild area in spring and the rest into seed trays, to give the young plants a head start.

Thin the seedlings out and plant strong young plants into the garden. Before planting take off any existing vegetation where the plants are to be set out to let the plants grow unhindered until they become established and large enough to fend for themselves.

Wildflower bulbs   Bulbs play an important part in the wildflower garden, providing color year after year and multiplying speedily. *Fritillaria meleagris*, the snake's head fritillary (zones 3-8), and dwarf narcissus will colonize meadow land. It is important that the grass isn't cut until after the bulbs' foliage has died down and the wildflowers have shed their seed.

Wildflower gardens should not be left to run riot. This is a carefully thought-out patch within a larger, well-maintained garden.
1. Poppies will multiply rapidly.
2. Alliums can be left to self-seed.
3. Rudbeckia (just coming into flower here) will supply a golden late-summer display when the poppies and alliums fade.

Five great wildflowers

Achillea millefolium (yarrow) Perennial
Centaurea cyanus (bachelor's button) Annual
Leucanthemum vulgare (ox-eye daisy) Perennial
Papaver rhoeas (field poppy) Annual
Primula veris (cowslip) Perennial

scented garden

Scented, aromatic, or perfumed — call them whatever pleases you — these are the plants that bring memories flooding back from childhood, when the days were hot and it never rained in summer. One whiff of sweet pea, lilac, lavender, or pinks, and you are transported back to the very garden. They say that you can't buy memories, but for the price of a pack of seed or a few dollars for a plant, you can not only have memories, but you can choose the ones you want.

Some scented plants are best known for their foliage, such as rosemary, sage, and prostanthera (mint bush). Planted close to paths, they release their aroma as you brush against them. Others rely on their flowers for scent, such as lily and lilac, while yet more are endowed with both scented flowers and foliage, good examples being lavender and choisya. Some give of their best after a shower in the evening, when a walk in the moonlight can bring you face to face with the heady perfume of night-scented stock.

Great scented plants

Choisya ternata (Mexican orange blossom) Shrub with scented flowers and leaves

Daphne mezereum Shrub with fragrant flowers

Lavendula stoechas (French lavender) Shrub with scented flowers and leaves

Perovskia atriplicifolia (Russian sage) Subshrub with aromatic leaves

Roses, especially the older varieties. Shrubs and climbers with scented flowers

Viburnum x carlcephalum Shrub with scented flowers

Lonicera fragrantissima (honeysuckle) Climber with scented flowers (zones 5-8)

Convallaria majalis (lily of the valley) Ground cover with scented flowers

Jasminum officinale (jasmine) Climber with fragrant flowers

Paths edged with lavender and a tunnel of roses lead you along a scented trail into the herb garden.

Mediterranean plants Many aromatic plants are Mediterranean and appreciate full sun and can tolerate drought conditions. The leaves give off their scent when the oils in the foliage are released. This occurs when temperatures are high. Pruning every year will encourage new growth with young foliage that performs better. Mediterranean species enjoy a soil that is well drained and of an open gritty texture. If your soil is heavy and poorly drained, a bed can be made with a lighter soil and raised to provide better drainage. Raising the planting area will also bring the plants with their flowers and foliage closer to the nose; raised beds are especially useful for gardeners in wheelchairs. Grow some of the scented plants in pots on the patio and in beds close to garden seats to enjoy the perfume.

It is possible to have scent in the garden every month of the year. A must for midwinter is *Sarcococca confusa*, the Christmas box, with its tiny white flowers that drench the surrounding area with fragrance.

foliage garden

First-time gardeners may be excused for shying away from foliage gardens and opting instead for flower color. Yet leaves can be dramatic and eye-catching. Leaves come in every shape, color, and size, making bold architectural structures that the gardener can rely on and use to highlight and frame flowering plants. Deciduous foliage often changes color with the seasons, giving of its best in fall when it changes spectacularly from green to red, purple, and gold.

For screening the garden for privacy or shelter, evergreen foliage comes into its own, with escallonia, berberis, and yew all in demand.

The song claims that there are 40 shades of green, and if so, you can have them all in the garden in a choice of matt or glossy. Ferns such as *Matteuccia struthiopteris*, the shuttlecock fern (zones 3-8), unfurl pale green leaves in spring that quickly grow to 6 ft (1.8 m). Then there are ornamental grasses such as miscanthus, some of which can grow to 10 ft (3 m) between spring and fall. Leaves are available in every color from green splashed with white — hostas are typical — to just about black, as with the low-growing, grasslike *Ophiopogon planiscapis* 'Nigrescens' (zones 6-10). Nature has allowed for gardeners with limited space by providing species that change their leaf color with the seasons.

Deciduous and evergreen plants may be used to complement one another; the bold, fingered, evergreen leaves of *Fatsia japonica* highlight the bare tracery of twiggy stems of *Betula jacquemontii*, while the glossy evergreen of holly can be mixed in a hedge of deciduous beech with its brown crinkly dead leaves and tightly wrapped, thin, pointed buds.

Rheum palmatum 'Atrosanguineum' has striking foliage that contrasts with the rounded leaves of *Ligularia dentata* 'Desdemona.'

Foliage comes into its own in winter when there is less flower color to compete and the leaves are suddenly highlighted. Flower arrangers fill their gardens with plants with odd-shaped leaves as essential backdrops to the flowers.

Five great foliage plants

Acer japonicum **'Vitifolium'** Deciduous tree for fall color

Hosta **'Wide Brim'** Perennial with green and white leaves

Rodgersia pinnata **'Superba'** Perennial with big divided leaves

Stachys byzantina Perennial with wooly leaves

Yucca gloriosa Perennial with swordlike leaves

Tip

Generally the best way to feed plants is to use a balanced fertilizer containing nitrogen, phosphate, and potash to encourage growth and flowering. If the foliage is the plant's main claim to fame, if you feed it with a high nitrogen fertilizer, the leaves will be larger, and there will be more of them.

herb garden

"Herb" is a collective term for a whole range of useful plants that are useful to us. There are culinary herbs, medicinal, strewing, and aromatic herbs, plus those used for herbal teas and for dyeing.

Unless you are feeding the five thousand, a small patch of herbs in the kitchen garden should suffice. If you want to make a feature of the herb area, you can create a knot garden, where small beds are kept separate by low hedges in a formal pattern. Dwarf box hedges are traditional but require regular clipping and are a great hiding place for snails. Lavender hedges are in keeping with the herbal theme and look attractive, but are short lived and need to be clipped every spring to encourage new growth from the base.

Herbs in containers Where only a few varieties are in demand, herbs can be grown in a container on the patio or outside the kitchen door for convenience. Before you head off to the garden center, give a bit of thought to which herbs you are likely to use, rather than buying a whole lot that you have heard of but will never get around to cooking with. Sage, rosemary, and thyme are well worth growing, as are parsley, mint, and bay. Mint is a bit of a thug and grown direct in a bed, it will spread all over the garden. It is best planted in an old bucket and plunged into the ground. Make sure the rim of the bucket is above soil level so the mint can't escape. One bay tree will produce more than enough leaves for culinary use. Unless you are into alternative medicine, don't bother with the medicinal herbs, as they will only take up space and never be used.

Plants grown in full sun in a well-drained, light gritty soil will reward you with the best flavor. When grown in containers, make sure there is good drainage by filling the bottom 4 in (10 cm) with large pieces of styrofoam. Cover them with horticultural fleece to stop the water from washing the soil down into the base and blocking the drainage holes. Use an open, free-draining soil and don't fill the pot to the top, leaving room to water.

For best flavor

Young new growths and leaves have the best flavor, so encourage growth on plants such as sage and thyme each spring by pruning. A light clipping is all that is needed rather than cutting into the older wood, which may not reshoot.

A top dressing of equal parts grit and peat worked into the center of woody species will encourage new roots to grow on the stem and rejuvenate the plant.

Avoid overfeeding herbs with nitrogen — and there is no need to enrich the soil with compost or manure at planting time. To make sure the soil is well drained, the herb garden can be planted in a raised bed in a sunny part of the garden, and creeping herbs such as thyme can be planted along the edge and allowed to grow over the sides and trail down.

Tip

It is possible to have fresh mint and parsley all winter if they are given some protection from the elements. When small amounts are adequate, grow them on the kitchen windowsill. In late fall dig a few roots of parsley and pot them in soil in a container deep enough to hold the long root. Trim off older leaves and water well. New growth will soon appear. The roots of the mint are just below the soil surface and can be lifted, laid on a shallow container, and covered with 1 in (2 cm) of soil and watered in. The new shoots will appear quickly and can be nipped off for use.

Five decorative herbs

Allium schoenoprasum (chives)
Borago officinalis (borage)
Lavandula stoechas (French lavender)
Rosmarinus officinalis (rosemary)
Thymus x citriodorus 'Bertram Anderson' (lemon thyme)

Clipped box hedges (1) contain the plants, leaving the gravel paths uncluttered. This showcase herb garden at the famous Ballymaloe Cookery School in Ireland contains, among many others, nasturtiums (2), sage (3), globe artichokes (4), fennel (5), and evening primrose (6).

tropical garden

Even in cooler climates, it is possible to give that tropical, lush look and enclosed feeling to part of the garden. Lots of leafy plants, shade, and moisture are essential for success, and the site needs to be sheltered and warm. Plants such as annual coleus (*Solenostemon*) with their wonderfully colored leaves are normally thought of as conservatory or house plants in my part of the world, but they can be moved outside in their containers for the summer. The "vacation" will do them good, and they will enjoy the conditions and provide that exotic look at the time when the garden is most in use.

Site A warm, sheltered part of the garden overhung with mature trees is ideal, but in a new garden it may be necessary to settle for a sunny corner protected from the wind and planted with large foliage plants to provide the future leaf canopy. Avoid low-lying areas; they are often

Tip

Fragrance hanging on the evening air will make the tropical garden a favorite area, so incorporate a seat, preferably made of cane or rattan, to reinforce the tropical feeling. If the site is sheltered, plant *Dregea sinensis* (zones 9-10), an evergreen climber that will provide all the fragrance necessary from its creamy white summer flowers.

frost pockets where the cold air drains down to the lowest part of the garden, damaging all but the hardiest of plants.

The soil needs to be free draining with no risk of waterlogging, but needs to retain enough moisture to encourage mosses and ferns to cover the tropical floor and some of the best of the less aggressive clematis, such as *C.* 'Dr Ruppel', to scramble about higher up among the other plants.

Planting There is always the risk of ending up with a jungle, and even a tropical jungle is to be avoided. Correct spacing of the plants is important, since warm, moist growing conditions will encourage rampant growth, allowing the more aggressive species to take over, smothering smaller plants and generally becoming a nuisance. Mulching the soil with composted leaves will not only help to retain moisture and deter weeds, but will also add to the aesthetics, providing that humid feeling.

Feeding To encourage the plants to produce leafy growth, feed a high-nitrogen fertilizer at two-week intervals during the summer. In the fall revert to high-potash fertilizer to harden the plants up for the winter.

The striking foliage of palm and banana raises the temperature in this deck in Melbourne, Australia.

Five great "tropical" plants

Echium pininana
Fatsia japonica
Ficus carica (common fig)
Gunnera manicata
Phormium tenax (New Zealand flax)

children's garden

There are two schools of thought: you can allow the children to have free run of the whole garden, or a portion of the garden can be set aside for their exclusive use. I am very much in favor of giving them part of the garden, but I suppose consideration has to be given to their age and how well behaved the children in question are.

If none of the garden is out of bounds, you must expect some damage to plants through youthful enthusiasm. It is not fair or enjoyable to be constantly shouting at them. And no matter how well behaved your own offspring are, their friends may be little horrors with no respect for property or plants.

The big advantage in giving an area over to the children is that when they are young you can fence them in and keep an eye on them at the same time. Choose an area close to the house within sight of the kitchen window for peace of mind. All the toys can be kept inside the play area, which makes grass cutting a simple task without having to clear the lawn before you start the mower.

Young gardeners Turning children into gardeners is every bit as pleasing as helping them to qualify in their chosen profession. Start them off with an area of ground that won't appear enormous, yet is large enough to grow a variety of plants. A 6 ft (2 m) square plot is ideal. Make sure it is free of any perennial weeds, and cultivate the soil to leave it in a condition to be worked with small hand tools.

Gardening has to be made interesting for children, with no early setbacks. A sure way to success is to encourage them to grow something they like to eat. Quick-growing food crops include sugar snap peas, radishes, early carrots, lettuce, and, best of all, strawberries. Plants that mature quickly are also satisying. Sunflowers from seeds are great fun: not only are there enormous 8 ft (2.5 m) high giants that need staking, there are dwarf sunflowers with large flowerheads.

Propagation has always interested children, provided they can see results fast. Sowing seeds, planting, and taking cuttings will all hold their attention if growing happens like magic. Seeds don't have to be sown in rows, but can form letters or the child's name. Hebes, especially 'Purple Queen,' and catnip will root like weeds. Cuttings will form small plants in about four weeks, grown outdoors in summer in a sandy soil, using a cut-down plastic drinks bottle as a miniature cloche.

Five easy plants for children

Tropaeolum majus (nasturtium)
Primula vulgaris (primrose)
Galanthus nivalis (snowdrop)
Fragaria x ananassa (strawberry)
Lathyrus odorata (sweet pea)

Tip

Pumpkins are great fun to grow from seed. If sown in May, they will be ready for Halloween. The way to produce large fruit is to grow the plant on a raised bed that is free draining, with lots of added compost, and restrict the crop to one pumpkin per plant.

Safety first

• Don't allow children to handle sharp tools.

• Don't allow children anywhere near mechanical or electrical equipment.

• Don't use any chemicals in the children's garden.

• Don't allow pets in the children's garden in case they use it as a sandbox.

• Don't grow poisonous plants or plants that can cause a skin allergy.

• Do insist that children wash their hands after working in the garden.

• Make sure the soil is free of broken glass and nails, and remove any stones larger than 2 in (5 cm) across.

The tissue-paperlike flowers are the main reason for growing poppies, but the seed heads are also eye-catching in dried flower arrangements.

growing tips for favorite plants

You don't have to be a gardener to have a favorite flower, but when you decide to grow your own, you become a gardener.

I have so many favorites, and as the seasons change, so does my loyalty. Some, such as roses, tend to be grown together in dedicated rose beds, while others, such as fuchsias, pop up here and there in mixed plantings. Clematis, too, may be dotted about, scrambling over fences, sheds, and old trees.

Giving your favorite what it likes by way of feeding, pruning, and soil type will undoubtedly make you its favorite, so take a tip from me…

clematis

There are small-flowered clematis and double-flowered clematis, spring-, summer-, fall- and even winter-flowering varieties; and while most of them are deciduous, there are some evergreen species, too. The majority of clematis are climbers, but there are some attractive herbaceous varieties that will stay at knee height. In other words, there are clematis to suit every taste and fill every niche in the garden.

Site and soil Most clematis dislike bitterly cold winds, preferring a more sheltered position. The exceptions are the small-flowered species such as *Clematis tangutica*, *C. alpina*, *C. montana*, and *C. macropetala* (all zones 6-9), which are tough and able to withstand all but the worst of conditions. All clematis do best in a reasonably sunny site, but can be grown in light shade; in fact, the pale-colored, large-flowered varieties fade in strong sunlight. As climbers they love to scramble up and over fences, trellis, sheds, and other trees and shrubs. Vigorous species such as *C. montana* are quite capable of climbing to the top of a 50 ft (15 m) tree.

Once they become established, clematis will grow successfully in most soils with the exception of

Group 1: *C. montana* 'Wilsonii'

Group 2: *C.* 'Vyvyan Pennell' and 'The President'

Group 3: *C. viticella* 'Abundance'

extremes of wet or dry, but they particularly enjoy a well-drained, moisture-retentive soil with lots of added farmyard manure, leaf mold, or compost. They prefer a cool root run, with their roots in the shade and well covered with a moisture-retentive mulch (see page 46 for suggestions). This will not only help keep the roots cool and prevent the soil from drying out in summer, it will also encourage the lower part of the stem to root into the compost.

Planting Since they are always sold as container-grown plants, clematis can be planted at any time without causing a check in the plant's growth. If you are planting in summer, water well afterward, since the plants will be in full growth.

Follow the step-by-step planting instructions on page 37. It is particularly important to place the rootball in the hole at least 4 in (10 cm) deeper than it was in the pot. This encourages extra roots to form on the stem and offers some protection against clematis wilt disease (see under Pests and Diseases, below). Protect the new young shoots from slugs and snails by using pellets or trapping them in containers of beer.

Pruning Newly planted clematis should be pruned in early spring just above the first pair of shoots. Nip out the tips of the resulting shoots to encourage them to form more sideshoots and branch out into a multistemmed plant. Clematis fall into three types, and after the first year, the pruning for each type is different.

Group 1 comprises *Clematis armandii, Clematis cirrhosa* (both zones 7-9), *Clematis alpina, Clematis macropetala,* and *Clematis montana.* Pruning is not necessary for any of these species, although if they have become too large or are taking over their support, they can be pruned as soon as flowering is finished. If the growth is a nuisance, cut them back hard and they will grow as if they had never been touched. If the plant is very large and mature, it may be best to spread this treatment over two or even three years.

Group 2 includes all the semi-double and double varieties and the early large-flowering types that flower before midsummer. They produce blooms on short growths and will often flower again in late summer and early fall. Some of the best known of this group are *Clematis florida* (zones 6-9), *C. lanuginosa* (zones 6-9), *C. patens.* (zones 5-9), and the varieties *C.* 'Nelly Moser' (zones 4-9), *C.* 'Lasurstern' (zones 4-9), and *C.* 'The

Group 1
Overgrown plants can be cut back after flowering. Remove weak or damaged growths and cut to reduce size.

Group 2
Prune in late winter to remove weak and damaged shoots, leaving a framework of strong, well-spaced shoots.

Group 3
Prune all shoots hard in late winter to 12 in (30 cm) above ground level. Remove dead shoots at ground level.

President' (zones 4-9).

Not a lot of pruning is needed for this group. At the end of winter, simply cut out dead bits and very thin, weak shoots, cutting just above a pair of nice plump buds. Don't prune too hard or the clematis won't produce its first flush of blooms. If the plant is totally overgrown, it can be cut hard after the first flush and the resulting new growths trained in to replace the old wood.

Group 3 includes *Clematis orientalis* (zones 6-9), *Clematis texensis* (zones 4-9), *Clematis viticella* (zones 5-9), and all the late large-flowering hybrids.

They all require severe pruning every year. They flower on the current year's growth so should be pruned hard in late winter. Look for the lowest pair of good strong buds on each main stem and cut just above them, removing everything that is growing beyond that. The plant will look butchered, but, believe me, you will have an abundance of flowers the same year.

Feeding All clematis appreciate regular feeding, and after pruning a balanced feed is needed to encourage the plant to produce strong, healthy shoots.

Pests and diseases Probably the worst pests are also the most common – slugs and snails play havoc with clematis in the spring, eating through the main young shoots. When you have cut hard back to the lowest buds and then lost them to slugs, it is a worry until new growth appears. During the season you can find snails 16 ft (5 m) up a wall or tree heading for the tops of your clematis.

Wilt disease of clematis is caused by the fungus *Ascochyta clematidina*. It attacks the tips of the plant first, then the leaf stalks turn black where they join the leaf and the young growths wither. Little research has been done on this problem, and there is no sure-fire method of prevention or cure. A deeper-than-average planting hole may help, and if the disease does strike, cutting the plant right back to ground level is the best remedy. Sometimes the plant will recover from lower down, producing shoots at soil level. If you have lost a clematis to wilt disease, don't plant another in the same spot.

Waterlogged soil and slug damage can also cause ordinary wilting, without these symptoms.

Other pests such as aphids and caterpillars can be a nuisance, but no more so than on other plants.

Growing in containers It is possible to grow clematis in a container, but it will need to be as large as possible, with extra drainage holes and a good moisture-retentive, soil-based medium. A large wooden barrel is ideal or any container that is at least 24 in (60 cm) deep and 18 in (45 cm) wide. The pot plus soil will be heavy, so position it out of direct strong sun before filling and planting. Leave the top 4 in (10 cm) of the container free of soil to allow for watering and applying a mulch each spring.

Clematis suitable for growing in containers include varieties of *C. alpina* and *C. macropetala* and *C.* 'Doctor Ruppel,' 'Vyvyan Pennell' (all zones 4-9) (a double-flowered variety), 'Miss Bateman,' and 'H F Young.'

Clematis armandii is evergreen and flowers in late winter with the exquisite scent of almonds.

roses

Roses have been with us for a very long time and have, over the centuries, adapted and changed with the times almost as well as the human race. Today, breeders and people dedicated to rose growing strive to bring us new, better, and more adaptable varieties to suit every situation in the garden. There are species roses, shrub roses, climbers, ramblers, cluster-flowered (floribunda), large-flowered bush (hybrid tea), patio, ground cover, and miniature roses. It really is not necessary to know or to grow all the different types, and the best advice I can give is to go out and buy the type of rose that is best suited to where you are going to plant it.

If a rose is to grow up a wall, trellis, or arch, choose a climber, rambler, or a vigorous shrub rose. Roses to be mass planted in a formal bed can be cluster or large flowered. Patio roses and miniature types do well in containers for the patio, and if there is a steep bank to be covered, some of the recently introduced ground-cover roses are ideal. Ultimate height and spread need to be considered: there are vigorous roses and there are rampant ones such as *Rosa filipes* 'Kiftsgate' (zones 6-9), which will grow up and along for 40 ft (12 m).

Some roses are almost evergreen, such as the Flower Carpet series (zones 5-9), with white, pink, red, and yellow in the range. When planting an island bed in a lawn, choose one variety of rose rather than a mixture of varieties in different colors that are bound to flower at different times. The perfume of a well-scented bloom is a heady aroma that

The highly scented gallica rose 'Charles de Mills,' with its fully double flowers, makes a fragrant summer shrub and can also be trained over a support.

never fails to bring back memories, and it is worth visiting some of the rose trial grounds in summer to check for yourself the fragrance of a particular rose. Some modern varieties have little or no scent, and breeders seem more interested in color, habit, or disease resistance than in what our noses want. Perhaps that is why many of the older perfumed roses are still available, while some of the more recent introductions have dropped out of the catalogs.

How to buy roses

There are two ways to buy roses; either as container-grown plants, which will not suffer a check in growth if planted carefully; then there are bare-root plants bought in the late fall, winter, or early spring. Bare-root plants can be purchased in garden centers, stores, direct from the nursery, or by mail order. They will have no leaves or flowers, but you will be able to see if the main roots are strong and healthy, and if there are lots of the small white fibrous roots that are essential for good growth. As soon as they arrive, take them out of any packaging and plant them. If the weather or the soil is not suitable for planting, the roses should be heeled into the ground as a temporary measure, so their roots are in close contact with damp soil and covered to prevent them from drying out. Choose a soil that is easily dug and firm the soil around the rose roots. When time and weather allow, put them in their permanent position, before the winter is over.

Pruning roses

Roses flower best on the young wood made that year: in other words, they flower on current growth. The principal of pruning roses is to remove the old wood and encourage new shoots. At pruning time you can also take the opportunity to remove dead, diseased, weak, and crossing stems, thereby keeping the plant healthy and less cluttered.

Rosa 'Arthur Bell,' cluster-flowered, double, yellow, and with a beautiful scent.

Good varieties

'Alex's Red' Fragrant, double red flowers, 36 in (90 cm) high (zones 5-9).

'Fragrant Cloud' Dark green leaves, very fragrant, large scarlet flowers, 30 in (75 cm) high (zones 5-9).

'Pot o' Gold' Very fragrant, double, golden-yellow flowers in clusters, 30 in (75 cm) high (zones 5-9).

'Arthur Bell' Bright green leaves, fragrant, double, buttercup-yellow flowers, 36 in (90 cm) high (zones 5-9).

'Evelyn Fison' Glossy, dark green foliage, double bright red flowers 28 in (70 cm) high (zones 5-9).

'Playboy' Glossy, dark green foliage, semi-double, orange-yellow flowers, 30 in (75 cm) high (zones 5-9).

Pruning large-flowered and cluster-flowered roses

When The most reliable time is in the spring, when the buds are swelling and can be clearly seen. In areas where there is less risk of frost, they can be pruned early; in colder climes it will have to be done later. In addition to spring pruning, established rose bushes are usually cut back by half in early winter, to reduce the risk of wind damage, which rocks the plant in the ground and injures the roots.

Where Cut out all damaged, dead, and diseased branches and any stems that are spindly. Cut with sharp shears and make a clean sloping cut about ¼ in (7 mm) above a bud.

How much Reduce all the main stems to about 8 in (20 cm) from the ground. For cluster-flowered roses where the size of individual blooms is not so important, the main shoots may be shortened to 10-12 in (25-30 cm). All prunings should be removed from the bed and burned to prevent the spread of diseases such as black spot.

Rosa complicata is a vigorous gallica rose that makes a sturdy and thorny hedge. It can reach a height and spread of 8 ft (2.5 m).

Pruning shrub roses

When Late winter is a good time to do the little pruning that is necessary to most of the shrub roses.

Where With the old-fashioned species roses, very little pruning is necessary. Simply cut out the very old wood, the dead branches, and any stems that are diseased. Modern shrub roses should be shortened back and tidied up.

How much The main shoots can be shortened by about one third.

Good varieties

'Charles de Mills' A gallica rose with quartered, fragrant double magenta-pink flowers in summer, 4 ft (1.2 m) tall (zones 3-9).

'Complicata' A gallica rose, vigorous, with large, single, pink flowers with pale pink centers, 8 ft (2.5 m) high (zones 4-9).

'Gertrude Jekyll' A modern shrub rose with large, double, deep pink, fragrant flowers in summer and fall, 5 ft (1.5 m) high (zones 5-9).

Rosa **'Dublin Bay'** is a trouble-free climber that can also be pruned to grow as a shrub.

Pruning climbers

When In fall when flowering is finished.

Where The old wood is cut out as close to the ground as possible without leaving a stump and any weak shoots removed. Thin out the main stems to form a framework that can be tied in, rather than let it become a tangle of branches. Cut the side shoots back in the fall.

How much The side shoots should be shortened by two thirds.

Good varieties

'Gloire de Dijon' A noisette rose with dark green foliage and quartered, double, fragrant, creamy-buff flowers in summer and fall, 16 ft (5 m) high (zones 6-9).

'Dublin Bay' Dark green leaves, double, bright crimson flowers in summer and fall, 8 ft (2.5 m) high (zones 5-9).

'Handel' Erect habit, dark green leaves, clusters of double, fragrant, cream flowers with deep pink edging, 10 ft (3 m) high (zones 5-9).

Rosa **'Félicité Perpétue'** is a joy to grow – vigorous, hardy, disease-free, and almost evergreen in mild gardens, it is still in flower later in the season than many other ramblers.

Pruning ramblers

When After flowering in late summer.

Where All the shoots that flowered should be cut out.

How much Only the new strong shoots that haven't flowered should remain, the old flowering shoots are cut out at ground level.

Good varieties

'Félicité Perpétue' Rosette-shaped, double pale pink to white flowers in summer, 16 ft (5 m) high (zones 6-9).

'Wedding Day' Rampant grower, single, fragrant, creamy-white flowers that age to pale pink in summer, 33 ft (10 m) high (zones 5-9).

rhododendrons and azaleas

The only thing that stops me from recommending that every garden should have one of these shrubs is their preference for an acid soil. Apart from that, there is something to suit every taste and every size of garden. Azaleas used to have their own genus, but are now classified as rhododendrons: the difference is that all rhododendrons are evergreen, whereas other azaleas are deciduous (though I can recommend the evergreen Kurume hybrids).

Rhododendrons tend to have large leaves and large flowers, while azalea flowers are smaller and appear in clusters. There are varieties that flower in the northern hemisphere as early as January – *Rhododendron* 'Christmas Cheer' (zones 6-8) seldom flowers for the festive season, but generally follows hard on its heels. A selection of varieties will provide a succession of blooms until early summer.

Plants range in size from the lovely little scarlet-flowered *Rhododendron forrestii* (zones 7-9) at 8 in (20 cm) to the towering 50 ft (15 m) high *R. macabeanum* (zones 8-10) with its 12 in (30 cm) leaves and huge trusses of deep yellow flowers, with contrasting purple blotches on the inside.

Many rhododendron hybrids have the excellent *R. fortunei* (zones 6-9) as one of their parents. Any that you come across are worth growing. This one, *R.* 'Fred Wynniatt,' grows to 13 ft (4 m) and can tolerate sun.

Soil and site Both rhododendrons and azaleas prefer a woodland situation in dappled shade, but will tolerate a more open site screened from the morning sun and shletered from cold winds. The soil must be well drained; the plants dislike waterlogged ground, enjoying moist conditions with added leaf mold and ericaceous medium. An acid soil with a pH of 4.5–5.5 is ideal. Rhododendrons are shallow rooted, and you can do a lot of damage by hoeing weeds around their base. To avoid this problem, a mulch of compost or bark will help keep the surface of the soil moist, cool, and weedfree.

Planting Dig a planting hole larger than the pot or rootball of the plant and fork up the base of the hole to assist drainage. If the soil is dry, prepare the planting hole the previous day, fill it with a bucket of water, and let it drain before planting. Add a handful of bonemeal to the soil as it is being replaced around the roots, and plant the rhododendron at the same depth as in the pot. Firm the soil around the rootball, and water well to settle the soil around the roots.

Pruning It is necessary to remove branches only to improve the shape of the plant or if they are crossing into the center of the shrub or rubbing together. Old straggly plants may be cut hard, and the branches will regrow from old wood. Deadhead after flowering to encourage growth rather than seed, taking care when removing the dead flowers not to damage the new shoots forming on each side.

Feeding An annual dressing of leaf mold in the spring is all that is needed. Take note of any foliage that turns pale yellow (chlorotic), since this is a symptom of a limy soil which does not give the plant enough iron or magnesium. In this case, apply these elements as a foliar feed.

Pest and diseases The only major pests are vine weevil larvae, which eat the roots, causing young plants to

R. 'Vuyk's Rosyred' (zones 6-8) is an evergreen dwarf azalea, ideal for a container. It flowers mid-spring and reaches 30 in (75 cm).

wither and die; and the adult weevils disfigure the foliage by eating the edges of the leaves.

Growing in containers All rhododendrons and azaleas do well in containers, but their main season of display is spring and early summer. The larger-growing species and hardy hybrid varieties will eventually outgrow the biggest container and need to be planted in the open, but until then they will give years of display. Check that there are lots of drainage holes in the base of the pot and that the soil is acidic and free-draining. Leave space at the top of the pot for watering and top-dressing.

fuchsias

The fuchsia is a plant for everyone. Young or old, male or female, gardener or non-gardener, most people are charmed by their flowers and by their easy cultivation. They can be grown as a pot plant or an outdoor shrub, although some varieties are not totally hardy in North America. They are available in the most wonderful choice of colors with flowers shaped like ballet dancers.

Soil and site Outdoors, fuchsias should be planted in a well-drained, fertile soil that retains moisture. They need full sun or partial shade in an area protected from biting cold winds. For indoor pot plants a loam-based medium is best, although they will succeed in a soilless medium provided it is not allowed to dry out. Position the plants in a bright place, but not in strong, direct sunlight.

Fuchsia **'Marinka' has red stems and red midribs to the leaves, and is excellent for a hanging basket.**

Planting Plant with the rootball 2 in (5 cm) deeper than in the pot and mulch every fall to protect the base from heavy frost. Apart from the hardy species such as *Fuchsia* 'Riccartonii' (zones 8-9) and *F.* 'Mrs Popple' (zones 7-9), most varieties die back to ground level in winter, reappearing in late spring when the young growths need protection from frost. I leave the dead woody stems as a marker.

Pruning Flowers are produced on young current season shoots, so prune hard in late spring to within a few buds of the older wood.

Feeding For outdoor shrubs, a general fertilizer may be applied in late spring at 1 oz (30 g) per sq yd. Give the hardy species a high-potash feed in the fall to firm up the wood before winter.

During the growing season, feed indoor plants every three weeks with a balanced liquid fertilizer. In winter, keep the watering to a minimum, but don't let the compost dry out completely or the plant roots will shrivel and die.

Pests and diseases This is where fuchsias lose brownie points. As pot plants they are susceptible to aphids, red spider mite, capsid bugs, and vine weevil. They also suffer from gray mold fungus disease. Outdoors they are not so vulnerable, with aphids being the main problem.

Growing in containers Fuchsias are great plants for hanging baskets and as center plants in larger containers. Varieties such as *F.* 'Cascade' (red and white), *F.* 'Hermiena' (purple and white), and *F.* 'Marinka' (red) are naturally trailing, and if they are fed every three weeks, they will drape baskets, hiding them completely.

F. **'Cascade,' a trailing variety with single flowers, can spread to cover a wall but needs to be protected from frost.**

Once you have identified some plants that appeal to you, you can have lots of fun combining them to create different effects. Mix flowers and foliage plants to provide variety and splashes of color, or choose several plants of the same color for a more subtle, harmonious look. Remember, your garden is a canvas on which you can paint any picture you like.

directory

This directory is a list of plants mentioned in How to Garden, with a description of the type of plant, its general appearance, and ultimate height.

It is by no means an exhaustive list of plants I could recommend, but it will start you off. You will soon realize that the fun of choosing plants is exceeded only by the joy of watching them grow to maturity.

Find yourself a good garden center with knowledgeable staff and pick their brains. They will welcome the chance to help you choose the right plant and will share in the pleasure of your success.

Acacia dealbata

Alcea rosea
'Chater's Double'

Allium schoenoprasum

Anthemis tinctoria
'E. C. Buxton'

Aquilegia vulgaris

Figures in brackets at the end of each entry indicate the zones — as described by the US Department of Agriculture — in which the plants are hardy (see page 17). Hardiness zones are not given for annuals.

Acacia dealbata (mimosa) Evergreen tree with hairy, fernlike, silvery green leaves and fragrant golden yellow flowers in winter and early spring. Grows best in a well-favored site or on a sheltered south-facing (north-facing in the southern hemisphere) wall. Height 50 ft (15 m). (9-10)

Acer (maple) Genus of mainly deciduous trees grown for fall color. **A. japonicum 'Vitifolium'** (Japanese maple) has broad, deeply lobed leaves coloring beautifully to brilliant red in fall. Mature trees seed freely. Height 16 ft (5 m). (5-7)
A. pseudoplatanus is the fast-growing common sycamore, with dark green leaves and yellow flowers in spring, followed by green winged seed. Height 100 ft (30 m). For more information on the many varieties of **Acer palmatum**, see page 170 (5-7)

Achillea (yarrow) Genus of ornamental perennials. **A. 'Coronation Gold'** is evergreen with silvery gray leaves and flat heads of small, golden yellow flowers in late summer and fall. Height 32 in (80 cm) (3-9). **A. filipendulina**, another evergreen, has gray-green leaves and flat, platelike, golden yellow flowerheads in summer and early fall. Height 4 ft (1.2 m). (3-9) **A. millefolium** is a wild flower. It is mat-forming with pungent pale green leaves and flattened yellowish-white and pink flowerheads in midsummer. Height 24 in (60 cm). (3-8)

Actinidia kolomikta Deciduous climber with dark green leaves tinged purple when young, developing white and pink variegations on the top half. Fragrant white flowers in summer, and female plants produce yellow-green fruit. Height 16 ft (5 m). (5-8)

Agastache foeniculum Perennial

with aniseed-smelling foliage, gray-green on the underside. Dense spikes of blue-violet flowers in summer and early fall. Height 40 in (1 m). (6-9)

Akebia quinata Semi-evergreen climber with dark green leaves, blue-green on the underside and tinged purple in the winter. Fragrant dark purple flowers appear in early spring, followed by 4 in (10 cm) long fruit. Height 33 ft (10 m). (5-9)

Alcea rosea Chater's Double Group (hollyhock) Vigorous perennial with pale green leaves and tall spikes of double flowers in early summer, in a range of colors including white, yellow, pink, red, and purple. Height 6 ft plus (2 m). (3-9)

Alchemilla (lady's mantle) Genus of perennials with sprays of small green or yellow flowers. **A. alpina** is mat-forming with deep green leaves, silver on the underside, and small greenish-yellow flowers in summer. Height 4 in (10 cm). (3-7) **A. mollis** is great for the front of a bed or the edge of a path. Its pale green, wavy-edged leaves hold drops of water like beads of mercury. It spreads rapidly but is easily kept in place. Height 18 in (45 cm), spread 24 in (60 cm). (4-7)

Allium cristophii. Bulbous perennial with strap-like gray-green leaves up to 18 in (45 cm) long. The leaves wither before the large 8 in (20 cm) umbels of up to 50 pink-purple, star-shaped flowers appear in early summer. Height 18-24 in (45-60 cm). (4-8). **A. schoenoprasum** (chives) has thin, hollow, dark green leaves, used as an herb, plus purple or white flowers in summer. Height 12 in (30 cm). (3-9)

Alnus cordata (Italian alder) Deciduous tree with glossy dark green leaves. Yellow-brown male catkins appear in late winter before the leaves. Height 80 ft (25 m). (5-7)

Amelanchier (snowy mespilus) Deciduous shrubs or trees with brilliant spring and fall leaf color. **A. canadensis** has white flowers in

spring, followed by small edible black fruit. (3-7) The leaves of **A. lamarckii** turn from copper to green and then brilliant orange and red in fall. Height 26 ft (8 m). (5-9)

Anthemis Perennials with daisylike flowers. **A. punctata subsp. cupaniana** has silvery green leaves turning gray-green in winter and white flowerheads in summer and early fall. Height 12 in (30 cm). (6-9) The flowers of **A. tinctoria 'E. C. Buxton'** are lemon yellow with deep yellow centers, excellent for cutting. Height 24 in (60 cm). (3-7)

Aquilegia vulgaris (granny's bonnet) Perennial with light green leaves, flowering in late spring and early summer in a range of cultivars and colors, from white to pink and blue to violet. Height 36 in (90 cm). (3-8)

Arbutus unedo (strawberry tree) Evergreen tree with shiny mid-green leaves and peeling, red-brown bark. The white flowers appear in fall at the same time as the rough-skinned red fruit from the previous year's blossom. Height 26 ft (8 m). (7-9)

Artemisia Evergreen shrubs with aromatic foliage. **A. arborescens** (wormwood) has ferny, silvery white foliage and small yellow flowers in summer and fall. Height 36 in (90 cm). (5-9) **A. 'Powis Castle'** has silvery gray leaves and panicles of silver-yellow flowers in late summer. Height 24 in (60 cm). (5-8)

Arum maculatum (lords and ladies, cuckoo-pint) Tuberous perennial with shiny green leaves. The flower is a greenish-yellow spathe or hood, with central purple-brown spadix in late spring, followed by spikes of red berries. Height 20 in (50 cm). (6-9)

Aster alpinus Spreading perennial with lance-shaped, mid-green leaves. The violet flowers 2 in (5 cm) in diameter appear in summer and have honey-yellow disc florets. Height 10 in (25 cm). (4-7) **A. novae-angliae 'Harrington's Pink'** (New England aster) is a deciduous perennial with mid-green leaves, flowering from midsummer until late fall with sprays of light pink, daisylike flowers with yellow centers. Height 4 ft (1.2 m). (4-8)

Astilbe Genus of deciduous perennials for moist soil in shade. In really wet, boggy conditions, astilbes prefer some sun. Remove the flowers of white varieties as soon as they have finished flowering since the dead flower spike looks unkempt. **A. x arendsii 'Fanal'** is one of my favorites, with dense panicles of deep red flowers in early summer. Height 24 in (60 cm), spread 36 in (90 cm). (4-9)

Aubrieta Low-growing, evergreen perennials that are spring flowering in shades of pink, mauve, and purple. Clip plants after flowering to keep them compact. They enjoy a sunny site. Height 2 in (5 cm). (5-7)

Aucuba japonica 'Crotonifolia' (spotted laurel) Evergreen shrub with glossy mid-green leaves speckled with bright yellow. It has small red-purple flowers in spring followed by red berries. Height 10 ft (3 m). (6-10)

Aurinia saxatilis Spring-flowering evergreen with gray-green foliage and yellow flowers. Plants need to grow in full sun. Height 8 in (20 cm). (4-8)

Berberis Genus of berried shrubs. **B. darwinii** is evergreen with glossy, dark green spiny leaves. It flowers in late spring with a mass of pendant clusters of orange flowers, followed by blue-black fruit. Height 10 ft (3 m). (7-9) **B. empetrifolia** is a spreading evergreen with spiny, dark green leaves, gray on the underside. Orange-yellow flowers appear in late spring, followed by shiny blue-black fruit. Height 18 in (45 cm). (7-9) **B. x stenophylla** has deep yellow flowers on arching branches in late spring, followed by blue-black fruit. It makes an impenetrable informal hedge. Height 10 ft (3 m). (6-9)

Bergenia 'Ballawley' (elephants' ears) Perennial with shining green

leaves turning red-purple in winter. Bright crimson flowers on red stems appear in late winter and last until late spring. Plants tolerate shade and leaf color is even better grown in poor soil. A good plant for winter; site it toward the front of the bed where it can be seen. Height and spread 24in (60 cm). (3-8)

Betula (birch) Deciduous trees with interesting bark. **B. pendula** (silver birch) has peeling, white-brown bark and mid-green leaves, turning yellow in fall. Pale brown male catkins are produced in spring. Height 80 ft (25 m). (2-7) The leaves of **B. pendula 'Youngii'** turn yellow in fall; after they drop, the twiggy, dome-shaped, "weeping" tree seems to crouch in the garden waiting for spring. (2-6)

Borago officinalis (borage) Annual with dull green, bristly foliage and star-shaped blue flowers in summer. Height 24 in (60 cm). (5-8)

Brachyglottis monroi Evergreen shrub whose leathery, olive-green foilage is white on the underside. Yellow, daisylike flowers are borne in summer. Height 36 in (90 cm). (9-10)

Buddleia davidii (butterfly bush) Deciduous, fast-growing shrub with gray-green leaves and long panicles of purple or lilac flowers in summer and fall. Height 10 ft (3 m). (6-9). **B. globosa** (orange ball tree) has deeply veined dark green leaves, 8 in (20 cm) long. Small, rounded clusters of fragrant orange and yellow flowers appear in early summer. Height 13 ft (4 m). (7-9, and best on the west coast of North America.)

Callistemon citrinus (crimson bottlebrush) Evergreen shrub with dark green leaves. Spikes of crimson-red flowers are produced in late spring and early summer. Plants are not fully hardy and dislike cold winds. Height 6 ft plus (2 m). (8-10)

Callistephus chinensis 'Ostrich Plume' (China aster) Annual with mid-green leaves and long-stemmed,

feathery double flowers in pink, red, crimson, and mauve in summer and fall. Height 24 in (60 cm).

Calluna (Scots heather or ling) Genus of evergreen perennials that range from small shrubs to ground cover. **C. vulgaris 'Darkness'** is a low-growing shrub with dark green leaves and short racemes of crimson flowers from late summer to early fall. Height 10 in (25 cm). **C. vulgaris 'H. E. Beale'** produces pale pink double flowers on long spikes in late summer and fall. The flowers are excellent for cutting. Height 16 in (40 cm). **C. vulgaris 'Kinlochruel'** has long clusters of double white flowers. Height 10 in (25 cm). (All 5-7)

Camellia Genus of evergreen shrubs with glossy green leaves and peonylike flowers. **C. x williamsii 'Donation'** has semi-double pink flowers in late winter and spring. Height 16 ft (5 m) high. (7-8) The leaves of **C. sasanqua 'Narumigata'** are paler on the underside; scented creamy white flowers flecked with pink appear in late fall. Height 16 ft (5 m). (7-8) **C. x williamsii 'Anticipation'** has double, deep red flowers in late winter and early spring. During frosty weather, direct early morning sun can destroy the flowers. Height 13 ft (4 m). (7-8)

Campanula Large genus of plants with bell-shaped flowers in summer. **C. glomerata 'Superba'** is a deciduous perennial with dark green leaves and violet-blue flowers clustered at the ends of stiff stems. Height 24 in (60 cm). (3-8) **C. persicifolia** is an evergreen perennial that forms rosettes of bright green leaves and has white to mid-blue, pendant flowers. Height 36 in (90 cm), spread 12 in (30 cm). (3-8)

Campsis x tagliabuana 'Madame Galen' Vigorous deciduous climber that clings to its support by aerial roots. The orange-red flowers are trumpet shaped and carried in panicles during late summer and fall.

Aster novae angliae 'Harrington's Pink'

Astilbe x arendsii 'Fanal'

Berberis darwinii

Bergenia ciliata

Callistemon citrinus

Campsis x tagliabuana 'Madame Galen'

Carya ovata

Cerastium tomentosam

Cercis siliquastrum 'Bodnantense'

Chaenomeles speciosa 'Moerloosei'

Height 33 ft (10 m). (5-9)

Carpenteria californica Bushy evergreen shrub with glossy, dark green leaves and peeling orange-brown bark. Cup-shaped, fragrant white flowers with bright yellow stamens appear in midsummer. Height and spread 6 ft plus (2 m). (8-9)

Carya ovata (hickory) Deciduous tree with peeling gray-brown bark and mid-green leaves that turn brilliant yellow in fall. It produces edible nuts. Height 65 ft (20 m). (4-8)

Caryopteris x clandonensis 'Kew Blue' Deciduous shrub with aromatic gray-green leaves and dark blue flowers in late summer and fall. Height 36 in (90 cm). (6-9)

Ceanothus Genus of both evergreen and deciduous shrubs – one of the few plants to produce genuinely blue flowers. Most varieties like a sunny site. **C. 'Puget Blue'** is an evergreen with deeply veined dark green leaves and profuse deep blue flowers in late summer. Height 13 ft (4 m). (8-10) **C. 'Italian Skies,'** also evergreen, has glossy, light green leaves and bright blue flowers in spring. Useful for ground cover, it spreads to 10 ft (3 m). Height 4 ft (1.2 m). (9-10)

Celmisia spectabilis (New Zealand daisy) Evergreen perennial with leathery, silvery green leaves, wooly on the underside. The large daisy flowerheads have white ray flowerets and bright yellow centers and are carried on long wooly white stems in early summer. Height 12 in (30 cm). (8-9)

Centaurea cyanus (bachelor's buttons) Classic meadow wild flower, annuals with mid-green leaves. They produce dark blue flowers with violet inner petals in late spring and early summer. Height 24 in (60 cm).

Centranthus ruber (red valerian) Short-lived perennial with mid-green leaves and fragrant funnel-shaped flowers in shades of white, pink, or deep red. Blooms from late spring to

late summer and likes a lime soil. Height 3ft (90 cm). (5-8)

Cerastium tomentosum (snow-in-summer) Rampant, mat-forming perennial with gray wooly leaves. Plants are covered in star-shaped white flowers in late spring and summer. Height 3 in (8 cm). (3-7)

Ceratostigma willmottianum Deciduous shrub with 2 in (5 cm) long, dark green, purple-margined leaves which turn red in fall. The clusters of mid-blue flowers are 1 in (2 cm) across in late summer and fall. Height 3 ft (1 m). (5-9)

Cercidiphyllum japonicum (Katsura tree) Deciduous tree. The mid-green leaves are bronze when young and turn yellow, orange, and finally red in fall, when they smell of burnt sugar. The color is best in an acid soil. Height 50 ft (15 m). (4-8)

Cercis siliquastrum (Judas tree) Deciduous tree with heart-shaped blue-green leaves that are bronze when young, turning yellow in fall. The deep purple-pink flowers appear in spring, before or with the young leaves. Height 26 ft (8 m). (6-9)

Chaenomeles (flowering quince, japonica) Spring-flowering, deciduous shrubs with fragrant fruits. **C. speciosa** has spiny branches and dark green leaves. Scarlet flowers appear in spring, followed by hard, yellow, aromatic fruit. Height 8 ft (2.5 m). (4-8) **C. s. 'Moerloosei'** has white flowers flushed dark pink, followed by yellow fruit in fall. Height 6 ft plus (2 m). (5-8) **C. x superba 'Crimson and Gold'** has mid-green leaves, spiny branches, and dark red flowers with golden anthers. Height 36 in (90 cm). (5-8)

Chamaecyparis (false cypress) Genus of evergreen conifers that vary in size. **C. lawsoniana** has a columnar shape and bright green leaves. Height 100 ft (30 m). (5-9) **C. pisifera 'Boulevard'** has peeling red-brown bark and soft bluish foliage. Height 33 ft (10 m). (4-8)

Choisya ternata (Mexican orange blossom) Evergreen shrub with aromatic, dark green foliage. Fragrant white flowers are produced in spring and again in early fall. Height 8 ft (2.5 m). (7-10)

Chrysanthemum (florists' chrysanthemum) Genus of perennials with flowers in a range of shapes. Either a spray or single heads of flowers are produced, depending on whether or not the plants were disbudded to leave only one bud to open. Available in a range of colors from late summer through until late fall. Height 3–5 ft (90–150 cm).

Cistus (sun rose) Genus of evergreen, summer-flowering, bushy shrubs with sticky leaves and shoots. (8-10)

Clematis see page 160.

Clethra Shrubs and small trees with spires of fragrant flowers. **C. alnifolia** (sweet pepper bush) is deciduous, with mid-green leaves and white flowers tinged pink in late summer and fall. Height 8 ft (2.5 m). (3-9) **C. delavayi** has deep blue-green leaves and cup-shaped white flowers. Height 13 ft (4 m). (7-9)

Clianthus puniceus 'Albus' (lobster claw) Evergreen shrub with dark green leaves that prefers a wall to scramble up. White flowers shaped like lobster claws appear in spring and early summer. Height 13 ft (4 m). (8-11)

Convallaria majalis (lily of the valley) Perennial that spreads by rhizomes. Pairs of dark green leaves and sprays of bell-shaped, fragrant, waxy white flowers appear in late spring. Height 8 in (20 cm). (2-7)

Cordyline australis (New Zealand cabbage palm) Evergreen tree with long, lance-shaped pale green leaves and large panicles of creamy white flowers in summer. As the tree matures, the lower leaves fall off, leaving a bare trunk. Height 33 ft (10 m). (10-11)

Cornus alba (dogwood) Deciduous shrub with red winter shoots and mid-green leaves. Small white flowers in late spring are followed by white fruit with a touch of blue. Height 10 ft (3 m). (2-8)

Corylus avellana (hazel) Deciduous shrub with mid-green leaves and yellow catkins in late winter and early spring. Height 13 ft (4 m). (3-9)

Cotinus 'Grace' (smoke bush) Deciduous shrub with purple leaves turning bright, translucent red in fall. Height 16 ft (5 m). (5-8)

Cotoneaster Genus of shrubs valued for their bright red berries in late summer and fall. *C. frigidus* 'Cornubia' is semi-evergreen with dark green leaves and white flowers. Height 20 ft (6 m). (6-8) *C. lacteus* is evergreen, and its dark green leaves are off-white on the underside. It makes an ideal informal hedge. Height 13 ft (4 m). (7-9)

Crataegus (hawthorn) Deciduous trees with glossy dark green leaves and fragrant flowers, generally white with pink anthers, in spring, followed by dark red fruit. *C. monogyna* is commonly grown as a field hedge as its thorns deter animals. Height 33 ft (10 m). (5-7) For a change, try a red-flowering variety such as *C. laevigata* 'Paul's Scarlet.' Height 16 ft (5 m). (5-8)

Crinodendron hookerianum (lantern tree) Evergreen shrub that prefers an acid soil. Lantern-shaped deep pink or scarlet flowers appear from late spring through summer. As it is not totally hardy, the young growths are often damaged by spring frosts. Height 20 ft (6 m). (9-10)

x *Cupressocyparis leylandii* 'Castlewellan' (golden Leyland) Fast-growing evergreen conifer with bright yellow foliage, used for formal or informal hedging. Will quickly reach 80 ft (25 m) if you let it. (6-9)

Cyclamen coum Tuberous perennial with leaves that are either plain deep green or have silver markings. Small white, pink, or red flowers appear in winter, at the same time as the foliage. Height 2 in (5 cm). (5-9)

Cytisus (broom) Genus of deciduous, semi-evergreen, or evergreen shrubs that should be pruned immediately after flowering. Depending on the species, flowering may take place any time from early spring to fall. *C. battandieri* (pineapple broom) is semi-evergreen with silver-gray leaves and pineapple-scented, clear yellow flowers in mid to late summer. Height 13 ft (4 m). (8-9) *C.* 'Lena' is deciduous and its yellow flowers have bright red "wings." Height 6 ft (1.8 m). (6-9)

Daboecia cantabrica 'Bicolor' Low-growing evergreen shrub with mid-green foliage and racemes of urn-shaped white, pink, and red flowers in separate colors on the same stem throughout summer and early fall. Height 12 in (30 cm). (6-7, and best on the west coast of North America.)

Dactylorhiza fuchsii (common spotted orchid) Deciduous meadow or woodland orchid with purple-spotted leaves. White, pale pink, or mauve flowers with deep red markings bloom in late spring and early summer. Height 18 in (45 cm). (5-8)

Daphne Deservedly popular genus of sweet-scented flowering shrubs, a number of which bloom in winter and very early spring, adding much-needed cheer to the garden. *D. laureola* (spurge laurel) is an evergreen shrub with shiny, dark green, leathery leaves. Clusters of yellow-green flowers appear in late winter and spring, followed by black fruit. Height 36in (90 cm). (7-8) *D. mezereum* is a very fragrant deciduous species that flowers in mid to late winter before the leaves appear. Height 4 ft (1.2 m). (5-8)

Delphinium 'Butterball' Herbaceous perennial with mid-green leaves and semi-double off-white flowers with a deep yellow center. Flowers are produced in early summer. Height 5 ft (1.5 m). (3-7)

Deutzia x hybrida 'Mont Rose' Deciduous, summer-flowering shrub with dark green leaves and starlike deep pink flowers with yellow stamens. Height 4 ft (1.2 m). (6-8)

Dianthus alpinus 'Joan's Blood' Herbaceous, cushion-forming perennial with dark green leaves. In summer the plant is covered with single, deep pink flowers with crimson centers and bearded, toothed petals. Height 3 in (8 cm). (3-7) *D. gratianopolitanus* (cheddar pink) is an evergreen perennial with gray-green leaves that produces single, deep pink, fragrant flowers in summer. Height 6 in (15 cm). (3-8)

Diascia rigescens Herbaceous perennial with small, heart-shaped leaves. Tall spikes of deep pink flowers are produced in summer and will flower continuously if you remove dead flower heads. Diascias are not hardy in cold areas. Height 12 in (30 cm). (7-9)

Dicentra formosa (wild bleeding heart) Deciduous perennial with mid-green basal leaves and long arching stems of pink flowers in late spring and early summer. Height 18 in (45 cm). (4-8)

Digitalis (foxglove) Genus of biennials or short-lived, summer-flowering perennials. *D. purpurea* has dark green leaves and tall, one-sided spikes of white, pink, or purple flowers speckled purple on the inside. Height 3-6 ft (1-1.8 m). (4-8) *D. purpurea* Excelsior Group make a great show with their mid-green leaves and tall spikes of yellow, white, pink, or purple flowers arranged all around each stem. Deadhead after flowering, removing the whole stem to prevent the plant

Choisya ternata

181

Cotoneaster frigidus 'Cornubia'

Crinodendron hookerianum

Delphinium 'Butterball'

Diascia rigescens

Mandevilla laxa

Nyssa sinensis

Olearia macrodonta

Paeonia
cambessedesii

Phlox stolonifera
'Home Fires'

spring, followed by small yellow fruit. Height 26 ft (8 m). (4-8)

M. tschonoskii has glossy mid-green leaves that turn purple, red, and orange. Its pink-flushed white flowers are followed by red fruit tinged with yellow and green. Height 26 ft (8 m). (5-8)

Mandevilla laxa (Chilean jasmine) Deciduous climber with dark green leaves and tubular, very fragrant white flowers in summer and early fall. Plants require a sheltered wall to survive. Height 10 ft (3 m). (10-11)

Meconopsis grandis (Himalayan blue poppy) see page 171. (5-8)

Mentha suaveolens '**Variegata**' (variegated pineapple mint) Vigorous spreading perennial with hairy, wrinkled, gray-green leaves splashed and margined with cream. The spikes of pink or white tubular flowers appear in summer. Height 24 in (60 cm). (6-9)

Monarda '**Cambridge Scarlet**' (bergamot) Herbaceous perennial with purple-green leaves and scarlet flowers with deep red calyces in late summer and early fall. Height 36 in (90 cm). (4-9)

Myosotidium hortensia (Chatham Island forget-me-not) Evergreen perennial with glossy, ribbed, bright green leaves and large clusters of mid-blue flowers in early summer. Height 24 in (60 cm). (8-9)

Myrtus communis (common myrtle) Evergreen shrub with dark green, aromatic leaves. The white flowers with prominent white stamens are produced in late summer and early fall. Height 10 ft (3 m). (8-9)

Nandina domestica (heavenly bamboo) Evergreen shrub with bright green leaves that are reddish-purple when young and turn back to the same shade in winter. Panicles of white flowers with yellow anthers in midsummer are followed by red fruit. Height 6 ft plus (2 m). (6-9)

Neillia thibetica Deciduous shrub with bright green leaves and arching sprays of bell-shaped, bright pink flowers in early summer. Height 6 ft plus (2 m). (6-9)

Nepeta x faassenii (catmint) Perennial with aromatic, silver-green, wrinkled leaves and spikes of mid-blue flowers with purple spots in summer and early fall. Height 18 in (45 cm). (4-8)

Nyssa sinensis (Chinese tupelo) Deciduous tree with bronze leaves turning deep green and then orange, yellow, and red in fall. Height 26 ft (8 m). (6-9)

Olearia macrodonta Evergreen shrub with hollylike, glossy, dark green leaves that are white felted on the underside. Fragrant white daisylike flowers with red-brown centers are borne in summer. Height 20 ft (6 m). (9-10)

Osmanthus delavayi Evergreen shrub with leathery, dark green leaves and tubular, fragrant white flowers in spring. Height 13 ft (4 m). (7-9)

Othonna cheirifolia Evergreen shrub with fleshy, pale green leaves and yellow daisylike flowers in summer. Height 12 in (30 cm). (8-9)

Pachysandra terminalis Evergreen perennial with shiny, dark green leaves and small white flowers in early summer. Height 8 in (20 cm). (4-8)

Paeonia (peony) Genus of herbaceous perennials with large single or double flowers in early summer. Watch out for slugs eating the stems. *P. lactiflora* '**Bowl of Beauty**' has mid-green leaves and semi-double, pink-red flowers with creamy white centers. Height 36 in (90 cm). (3-8) *P. cambessedesii* has dark green leaves with purple veins and purple under-sides. Its bowl-shaped flowers are deep pink with yellow stamens and red filaments. Height 18 in (45 cm). (7-8)

Papaver orientale see page 171. (4-9).

Parrotia persica (Persian ironwood) Brilliant tree for fall color, with glossy green leaves that flush yellow, orange, and purple. The flowers are red, appearing in tiny clusters in late winter before the leaves. Height 23 ft (7 m). (4-7)

Parthenocissus henryana (Virginia creeper) Deciduous climber with dark green leaves veined with white. The leaves turn red in fall. Height 40 ft (12 m). (6-8)

Paulownia tomentosa (foxglove tree) Deciduous tree with large bright green leaves and panicles of fragrant lilac flowers marked with purple and yellow on the inside. The fawn feltlike buds develop in the fall and overwinter, opening in late spring. Height 33 ft (10 m). (5-8)

Perovskia (Russian sage) Subshrubs with gray-white shoots and gray-green aromatic leaves. *P. atriplicifolia* has spires of small violet-blue flowers in summer and early fall. Height 4 ft (1.2 m). (6-9) *P.* '**Blue Spire**' is deciduous and has violet-blue flowers in late summer and fall. Height 4 ft (1.2 m). (6-9)

Persicaria bistorta '**Superba**' Evergreen perennial with dark green leaves turning red-bronze in fall. Flowering from summer to fall, the spikes of rose-red flowers fade to pink and finally become brown in winter. Height 10 in (25 cm). (4-8)

Philadelphus (mock orange) Genus of deciduous shrubs with dark green leaves and very fragrant flowers. *P.* '**Belle Etoile**' has single, cup-shaped white flowers with purple markings in the center in late spring and early summer. Height 4 ft (1.2 m). (5-8) *P.* '**Virginal**' has double white flowers in midsummer. Height 10 ft (3 m). (5-8)

Phlomis fruticosa (Jerusalem sage) Evergreen shrub with gray-green leaves and mustard-yellow flowers in early summer. Height 36 in (90 cm). (8-9)

Phlox Genus of colorful perennial and annual flowering plants. The two listed are perennials. *P. stolonifera* (creeping phlox) has dark green leaves and pale to deep purple flowers in early summer. Height 4 in (10 cm). (4-8) *P. subulata* is evergreen, flowering in late spring and early summer in shades of white, pink, purple, and red. Height 6 in (15 cm). (3-8)

Phormium tenax (New Zealand flax) Perennial with stiff upright leaves up to 10 ft (3 m) long, dark green on the upper surface and blue-green on the underside. Panicles of red-brown flowers on 13 ft (4 m) stems in summer. (8-10)

Picea glauca var. albertiana 'Conica' Slow-growing conifer, cone-shaped with pale green foliage. Eventual height 16 ft (5 m). (3-6)

Pieris Genus of evergreen shrubs that flower in late winter and spring. *P. 'Forest Flame'* has shiny, dark green leaves that are brilliant red when young, turning pink and then green. Sprays of white flowers appear in spring. Height 6 ft plus (2 m). (7-9) *P. japonica* has glossy mid-green leaves and sprays of white flowers in late winter. Height 13 ft (4 m). (6-8)

Pinus nigra (Austrian pine) Evergreen conifer with pairs of dark green leaves and 3 in (8 cm) long cones. Height 100 ft (30 m). (5-8)

Pittosporum Evergreen shrubs and trees flowering in late spring and early summer, with scented flowers. *P. tenuifolium* forms a shrub or small tree with glossy, mid-green leaves with wavy margins. Small, honey-scented, dark red flowers are followed by black capsules. Height 33 ft (10 m). (9-10) *P. tobira* (Japanese mock orange) has leathery, deep green leaves and creamy white, bell-shaped flowers, followed by brown capsules and red seed. Height 16 ft (5 m). (8-10)

Polypodium vulgare (common polypody) Evergreen fern with leathery, dark green fronds. Height 12 in (30 cm). (6-8)

Populus (poplar) Deciduous, fast-growing tall trees. *P. alba* (white poplar) has dark green leaves with white undersides, turning yellow in fall. In spring male catkins are red and female are green. Height 100 ft (30 m). (4-9) *P. balsamifera* (balsam poplar) has balsam-scented buds and glossy dark green leaves, pale green on the underside. The green catkins appear in early spring. Height 100 ft (30 m). (5-9)

Potentilla fruticosa 'Elizabeth' Deciduous shrub with mid-green leaves and bright yellow flowers in summer and early fall. Height 36 in (90 cm). (3-7)

Primula Perennial plants, spring and summer-flowering. Those listed are fragrant. *P. florindae* (giant cowslip) is deciduous with long mid-green leaves and umbels of tubular, sulfur yellow flowers on long stems in summer. Height 36 in (90 cm). (3-8) *P. veris* (cowslip) is deciduous with mid-green leaves and umbels of deep yellow flowers in spring. Height 12 in (30 cm). (3-8) *P. vulgaris* (primrose) is evergreen with bright green leaves and pale yellow flowers in late winter and early spring. Height 8 in (20 cm). (4-8)

Protea cynaroides (king protea) Evergreen shrub with gray-green leaves and deep red or pink bowl-shaped flowers. Height 5 ft (1.5 m). (9-10)

Prunus (ornamental cherries and cherry laurels) Genus of trees that are covered with blossom in spring or summer. *P. 'Amanogawa'* has upright branches clothed in semi-double, fragrant, pale pink flowers in spring and good fall leaf color. The stiff branches resist wind damage, so the blossom stays on the tree instead of becoming confetti just when the show is at its best. Height 15 ft (4.5m). (6-8) *P. laurocerasus* (laurel, cherry laurel) is an evergreen shrub with glossy, dark green leaves, pale green on the underside. Fragrant white flowers in late spring are followed by red fruit that turns black. An ideal plant for formal or informal hedging. Height 25 ft (8 m). (6-9) *P. sargentii* is deciduous. Its dark green leaves are red when young and turn bright red in early fall. The flowers are pale pink and produced in spring. Height 50 ft (15 m). (5-9) *P. spinosa* (blackthorn, sloe) forms a deciduous shrub or tree with spines and deep green leaves. White flowers appear before the leaves in early spring, followed by black, edible fruit. Height 16 ft (5 m). (5-9) *P. x subhirtella 'Autumnalis'* will brighten your day in the dead of winter. It produces semi-double white flowers tinged with pink in mild weather from fall through winter and into spring. Height 26 ft (8 m). (6-8)

Pseudopanax ferox Evergreen tree with long, thin, sharply pointed and toothed bronze-green leaves 18 in (45 cm) long. Panicles of green flowers are produced in late summer. Height 16 ft (5 m). (8-10)

Pulmonaria saccharata (Jerusalem sage) Evergreen perennial with white-spotted mid-green leaves. It flowers in late winter and early spring with white, violet, or red flowers with green calyces. Height 12 in (30 cm). (4-8)

Pulsatilla vulgaris (pasque flower) Deciduous perennial with light green leaves and bell-shaped, silky, pale pink or purple flowers in spring. Height 8 in (20 cm). (5-7)

Pyracantha Genus of evergreen shrubs with yellow, orange, or red berries in fall and winter and white flowers in spring. All species are thorny and grow well against a wall. Height up to 15 ft (4.5m). (6-9)

Quercus rubra (red oak) Deciduous tree with dull dark green leaves that turn red, brown, yellow,

Pieris 'Forest Flame'

18

Potentilla fruticosa 'Elizabeth'

Primula veris

Protea cynaroides

Pyracantha 'Orange Glow'

Rodgersia pinnata
'Superba'

Romneya coulteri

Rudbekia fulgida

Sarcocca confusa

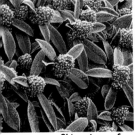

Skimmia confusa
'Kew Green'

and orange in fall. Height 100 ft (30 m). (5-9)

Rheum palmatum **'Atrosanguineum'** (Chinese rhubarb) Perennial with thick leaf-stalks and large crimson leaves emerging from red buds and aging to dark green. Large panicles of deep pink flowers appear in early summer. Height 8 ft (2.5 m). (5-9)

Rhododendron see page 172.

Rhodotypos scandens Deciduous shrub that dislikes heavy shade. It has deep green, heavily veined leaves and produces white, four-petaled flowers in spring and early summer, followed by shiny black berries. Height 5 ft (1.5 m). (5-8)

Rhus typhina **'Dissecta'** (stag's horn sumac) Deciduous shrub with velvety red shoots and dark green leaves turning orange-red in fall, when it also produces crimson fruit. Height 10 ft (3 m). (3-8)

Rodgersia pinnata **'Superba'** Clump-forming perennial with heavily veined, dark green leaves, tinted bronze when young. It produces tall plumes of pink flowers in late summer. Height 4 ft (1.2 m). (5-8)

Romneya coulteri (tree poppy) Deciduous subshrub that dislikes cold winds. It has glaucous gray-green leaves and large pure white, tissue-paperlike flowers with prominent orange-yellow stamens, which are produced all summer. Height 6 ft plus (2 m). (7-8)

Rosa eglanteria Deciduous shrub with prickly stems and aromatic, dark green leaves that smell of apples, especially after rain. The summer-flowering, single, rose-pink blooms have no perfume. They are followed by deep red hips in fall. Height 8 ft (2.5 m). (4-8). For other roses, see page 163.

Rosmarinus officinalis (rosemary) Evergreen shrub with aromatic, narrow, dark green leaves and deep blue to white flowers, which are

produced in late spring and early summer and again in fall. Height 4 ft (1.2 m). (7-10)

Rudbeckia Perennials and annuals with daisylike flowers. *R. fulgida* (black-eyed Susan) is a perennial with mid-green, hairy leaves and orange-yellow flowerheads with dark brown centers in late summer and fall. Height 36 in (90 cm). (4-9) The dark green foliage of *R. f.* **var.** *sullivantii* **'Goldsturm'** is a contrast to the large golden yellow flowers, each with a dark brown buttonlike center. This perennial flowers from midsummer until late fall and likes a well-drained soil. Height and spread 24 in (60 cm). (4-9)

Ruta graveolens **'Jackman's Blue'** (rue) Evergreen subshrub with aromatic, glaucous, blue-green foliage and yellow flowers in summer. Height 36 in (90 cm). (5-9)

Sambucus (elder) Deciduous shrubs or trees producing autumn berries. *S. nigra* **'Aureomarginata'** has yellow-edged, dark green leaves and musk-scented white flowers in early summer. Height 16 ft (5 m). (6-8) *S. n.* **'Guincho Purple'** (black elder or bour tree) has dark green leaves turning purple in late summer. Scented, pink-tinged flowers on purple stalks are produced in early summer. Height 10 ft (3 m). (6-8)

Santolina Small evergreen aromatic shrubs that flowers in summer. *S. chamaecyparissus* (cotton lavender) has gray-green leaves and bright yellow flowers on thin stems. Height 24 in (60 cm). (6-9) *S. rosmarinifolia* has bright green foliage and yellow flowers. Height 60 cm (24 in). (6-9)

Sarcococca (sweet box) Evergreen shrubs with fragrant white flowers in winter, followed by black fruit. All have glossy green leaves. *S. confusa* is the tallest, reaching 6 ft plus (2 m). (6-9) *S. hookeriana* spreads by suckering. Height 5 ft (1.5 m). (6-9) *S. h.* **var.** *humilis* is a dwarf,

suckering shrub with pink-tinged flowers. Height 24 in (60 cm). (6-9)

Skimmia Evergreen shrubs flowering in late spring. *S. x confusa* **'Kew Green'** has mid-green leaves and creamy white fragrant male flowers. Height 6 ft plus (2 m). (6-9)

S. japonica **'Fructu Albo'** has dark green leaves and green flower buds followed by white fruit. Height 24 in (60 cm). (7-9)

Sophora davidii Deciduous shrub with gray-green pinnate leaves and 6 in (15 cm) racemes of purple and white flowers in late spring and early summer. Height 8 ft (2.5 m). (6-9, best on the west coast of North America.)

Sorbus Deciduous trees with fall foliage and colorful berries. *S. aucuparia* (rowan, mountain ash) has dark green leaves that turn red or yellow in fall. White flowers in late spring are followed by orange-red berries. Height 50 ft (15 m). (4-7) *S. aria* **'Lutescens'** (whitebeam) has silvery gray young foliage that turns gray-green. White flowers in spring are followed by dark red berries. Height 33 ft (10 m). (6-8) *S. sargentiana* has sticky mahogany-colored buds in winter, followed by large, deep green, pinnate leaves that turn spectacular red and orange in fall. The fruit hangs in large deep red clusters. Grows slowly, but will eventually reach 33 ft (10 m). (5-7) The arching branches of *S. vilmorinii* are weighed down with dark red berries that turn pink and finally pure white. The small pinnate leaves don't color in fall, but form a good backdrop for the fruit. Height 15 ft (4.5 m). (6-8)

Spiraea Spring- and summer-flowering deciduous shrubs with starry flowers. *S.* **'Arguta'** (bridal wreath) has bright green leaves and white flowers in spring. Height 6 ft plus (2 m). (5-8) *S. japonica* **'Gold Flame'** has bronze and red young leaves, becoming yellow and finally green, plus deep pink flowers in summer. Height 36 in (90 cm). (4-9)

Stachys byzantina (formerly known as *S. lanata*; lambs' ears) Perennial with white wooly leaves and wooly pink-purple flowers from summer to early fall. Likes a well-drained soil in full sun. Forms a useful ground-covering mat. Height 18 in (45 cm) high, spread 24 in (60 cm). (4-8)

Syringa (lilac) Deciduous shrubs or small trees with fragrant flowers in late spring and early summer. **S. vulgaris** has mid-green leaves and conical clusters of mauve flowers. There are many named varieties producing single and double flowers in white, pink, blue, violet, and mauve. Height 20 ft (6 m). (4-8) **S. meyeri var. spontanea 'Palibin'** forms a dense shrub with pale pink flowers. Height and spread 5 ft (1.5 m). (4-7)

Tamarix ramosissima (tamarisk) Deciduous shrub with red stems and pale green leaves and sprays of pink flowers in late summer and early fall. Height 13 ft (4 m). (3-8)

Taxus baccata (yew) Evergreen conifer with dark green leaves and red fruit in fall. Makes a good formal or informal hedge. Height 33 ft (10 m). (7-8)

Thuja (cedar) Evergreen conifers. **T. occidentalis** (white cedar) has apple-scented pale green leaves and orange-brown bark. Height 50 ft (15 m). (2-7) The cultivar **'Rheingold'** is slow-growing, eventually reaching 6 ft plus (2 m) with a conical shape and pale green foliage. (2-7) **T. plicata** (western red cedar) has mid to dark green leaves that are pale green on the underside. It is useful for formal or informal hedging. Height 65–100 ft (20–30 m). (6-8)

Thymus (thyme) Evergreen subshrubs and herbs with aromatic leaves that do best in full sun. **T. x citriodorus 'Bertram Anderson'** has lemon-scented, gray-green and yellow leaves and pale lavender-pink flowers in summer. Height 12 in (30 cm). (6-9)

T. vulgaris has gray-green leaves and purple or white flowers in spring and early summer. Height 12 in (30 cm). (4-9)

Tolmiea menziesii (piggyback plant) Herbaceous perennial with pale green leaves with prominent veins. Unusually, young plants form on the leaves where the leaf and stalk meet. In late spring and early summer the plant produces scented flowers with green sepals and deep purple petals. Height 18 in (45 cm). (6-9)

Trachelospermum jasminoides (star jasmine) Evergreen climber with shiny dark green leaves turning red in winter. Fragrant white flowers are produced in late summer. Height 33 ft (10 m). (7-10)

Tropaeolum majus Gleam Hybrids (nasturtium) Trailing annuals with mid-green leaves and semi-double orange, yellow, and red flowers in summer and fall. Height 18 in (45 cm).

Ulex europaeus 'Flore Pleno' (gorse, whin, furze) Evergreen shrub with spine-tipped shoots and dark green leaves. The bright yellow double flowers are coconut scented and flower for most of the year. This variety doesn't set seed so, unlike the common gorse, it won't spread far and wide. Height 6 ft plus (2 m). (6-8)

Umbellularia californica (headache tree) Evergreen tree with aromatic mid-green leaves and pale yellow flowers in winter and spring. The crushed leaves can sometimes cause nausea and headaches. Height 50 ft (15 m). (7-9)

Verbascum chaixii 'Album' (nettle-leaved mullein) Semi-evergreen perennial with mid-green basal leaves and tall spikes of white flowers with mauve centers in late summer. Height 36 in (90 cm). (5-9)

Viburnum Easy-to-grow shrubs with white flowers. **V. carlcephalum** is deciduous with dark green leaves turning red in fall and fragrant flowers opening from pink buds in late spring. Height 10 ft (3 m). (6-8) **V. tinus** (laurustinus) is evergreen, with dark green leaves. It flowers in late winter and spring, followed by blue-black fruit. Height 10 ft (3 m). (8-10)

Vinca (periwinkle) Trailing plants for ground cover. These two species are evergreen and are great in dry shade under trees. **V. major 'Variegata'** has mid-green leaves edged with creamy white. Deep blue flowers appear from late spring until fall. Height 18 in (45 cm). (7-10) **V. minor 'Azurea Flore Pleno'** (lesser periwinkle) has dark green leaves and double, sky blue flowers in spring, summer, and fall. Height 4 in (10 cm). (4-9)

Viola Large genus of small flowering plants that includes a number of species of perennial violets. **V. cornuta** (horned violet) is evergreen with pale green leaves and fragrant violet blue and white flowers during spring and summer. Height 6 in (15 cm). (7-9) **V. labradorica** (Labrador violet) is semi-evergreen. Its dark green leaves are bronze when young and it has pale purple flowers in spring and summer. Height 3 in (8 cm). (2-8)

Weigela Deciduous shrubs in a range of cultivars with green, bronze, or variegated foliage and summer flowers in yellow, pink, cerise, red, and purple. Height 6–10 ft (1.5–3 m). (5-8)

Yucca gloriosa (Spanish dagger) Evergreen shrub with stiff, pointed, blue-green leaves and panicles of bell-shaped creamy white flowers in late summer and fall. The leaves of **Y. g. 'Variegata'** have yellow margins and its flowers, which appear in fall, are sometimes purple tinged. Height 6 ft plus (2 m). (7-10)

Zantedeschia aethiopica (arum lily) Perennial with bright green leaves. Its flowers are large white spathes with creamy yellow spadices, produced in late spring and early summer. Height 36 in (90 cm). (8-10)

Tamarix ramosissima

Tolmiea menziesii

Viburnum carlcephalum

Vinca major 'Variegata'

Zantedeschia aethiopica

index

192

index

Acknowledgements

The publishers would like to thank Charlie Ryrie for her contribution to the text and Steve Wooster for his glorious photography. Thanks also to Garden Picture Library, Unit 12, 35 Parkgate Road, London SW11 4NP, tel +44 (20) 7228 4332, fax +44 (20) 7924 3267 for their assistance, and to Chris Ellis of the Forest Lodge Garden Centre, Holt Pound, Surrey, for allowing us to take photographs there.

SW: Steven Wooster; GPL: Garden Picture Library; HA: Heather Angel; Holt: Holt Studios International Ltd

Page 1 GPL/Juliette Wade; 2/3 SW; 4 SW (Woodstock Garden, NZ); 5 SW (Bellevue Gardens, NZ, designed by Vivien Papich); 7 SW (Ian Fryer's garden, Christchurch, New Zealand); 8 GPL/John Glover; 9 SW (Forest Lodge); 10 Holt/Alan & Linda Detrick; 15 GPL/Michael Howes; 16 SW (design by Ton Ter Linden); 19 S & O Mathews; 20 GPL/Howard Rice; 23 SW (Old Vicarage, Norfolk); 27 Holt/Alan & Linda Detrick; 29 SW (Butterfly Conservation, Chelsea Flower Show 1998); 30 GPL/Jacqui Hurst; 34 Holt/Primrose Peacock; 38 SW (Saddlecombe); 39 GPL/Jerry Pavia; 41 SW (Bourton House Garden); 42/43 Heather Angel (Fisons Roof Top Garden, Chelsea Flower Show 1992, designed by Gillian Temple Associates); 44 SW; 47 SW (Bellevue Gardens, NZ, designed by Vivien Papich); 50 GPL/Clive Nichols; 51 GPL/Lamontagne; 52 GPL/Howard Rice; 53 David Beeson; 54 David Beeson (Longmead House); 55 GPL/Bob Challinor; 56 GPL/Neil Holmes; 59 GPL/Howard Rice; 60 GPL/Howard Rice; 62 top Holt/Nigel Cattlin; 62 bottom GPL/J S Sira; 63 top HA; 63 centre Holt/Len McLeod; 63 right HA; 63 bottom GPL/Christopher Fairweather; 64 left GPL/Sunniva Harte; 64 centre Holt/Nigel Cattlin; 64 right SW; 65 left HA; 65 centre GPL/ Lamontagne; 65 right GPL/Vaughan Fleming; 66 top left GPL/Michael Howes; 66 bottom left GPL/Howard Rice; 66 centre GPL/Neil Holmes; 66 right GPL/Michael Howes; 67 left GPL/Michael Howes; 67 centre HA; 67 right Holt/Nigel Cattlin; 68 left Holt/Nigel Cattlin; 68 centre GPL/Mel Watson; 68 right GPL/Lamontagne; 69 SW (Groombridge Place); 71 GPL/J S Sira; 73 GPL/Brigitte Thomas; 74 GPL/Andrea Jones; 75 SW (The Old Vicarage, Norfolk); 76 SW (Mount Usher); 77 SW (Garrets garden, New Zealand); 78 SW (Turn End); 80 SW; 83 top Gill McAndrew; 83 bottom SW; 84 SW (Boardman garden); 86 SW (the garden of Camilla Ross, London); 87 GPL/John Glover; 89 SW (design: Piet Oudolf); 90 Marianne Majerus; 91 SW (Yazdi garden, Holland, designed by Piet Oudolf); 93 GPL/Howard Rice; 94 GPL/John Glover; 96/97 SW (Ian Fryer's garden, Christchurch, New Zealand); 98 GPL/Alec Scaresbrook; 99 GPL/Alec Scaresbrook; 100 SW (Pauline Thompson's garden); 102 SW (Kilmokea, Co Wexford, Ireland); 103 SW; 104 top GPL/Lynne Brotchie; 104 bottom GPL/J S Sira; 105 SW (Hyde/Bennett garden); 107 SW (Himeji Japanese garden, Adelaide, Australia); 108 GPL/Neil Holmes; 110 SW (Glenbervie); 112/113 SW; 115 SW (design: Rod Barnett); 116 SW (Little Court, Crawley, Hants); 117 GPL/Didier Willery; 118 GPL/Juliette Wade; 119 GPL/John Glover; 120 Holt/Primrose Peacock; 121 SW (Japanese garden in Auckland, NZ, designed by Ted Smyth); 122 GPL/J S Sira; 123 GPL/Brigitte Thomas; 124 GPL/John Glover; 125 SW (Thijssehof); 127 Marianne Majerus; 128 SW; 129 GPL/Neil Holmes; 130 GPL/Brian Carter; 131 GPL/Michael Howes; 132 GPL/Georgia Glynn-Smith; 133 GPL/J S Sira; 135 SW (designed by Antony Paul); 137 GPL/Steven Wooster; 138 SW (Old Vicarage, Norfolk); 139 SW (Congham Hall); 141 SW (Chelsea Flower Show, design by Rupert Golby); 142 GPL/Zara McCalmont; 143 SW (the garden of Ross and Paula Greenville, Mt Manganui, NZ); 144 SW (Diana Firth's garden, NZ); 145 SW (Knockcree, Co. Dublin); 146 HA; 147 SW (Saling Hall); 148 SW (Old Vicarage, Norfolk); 150 SW (Old Rectory, Sudborough); 151 SW (Steven Wooster's garden) 152 GPL/Christi Carter; 155 SW (Ballymaloe); 156 GPL/Ron Sutherland; 159 HA; 160 top GPL/John Glover; 160 centre GPL/Linda Burgess; 160 bottom GPL/Howard Rice; 162 GPL/J S Sira; 163 GPL/Ron Evans; 164 left GPL/Roger Hyam; 164 right GPL/Mayer/Le Scanff; 165 left GPL/Marie O'Hara; 165 right GPL/Eric Crichton; 167 HA; 168 GPL/Mark Bolton; 169 GPL/John Glover; 170 GPL/J S Sira; 171 GPL/Howard Rice; 172 GPL/Brian Carter; 173 Holt/Nigel Cattlin; 174 GPL/Sunniva Harte; 175 Holt/Gordon Roberts; 177 SW (Ten ter Linden); 178 top to bottom: GPL/Gary Rogers, GPL/Howard Rice, GPL/Erika Craddock, Nicola Stocken Tomkins, GPL/Densey Clyne; 179 top to bottom: GPL/Brian Carter, GPL/Jacqui Hurst, David Beeson, David Beeson, GPL/Steven Wooster; 180 top to bottom: GPL/John Glover, GPL/John Glover, GPL/Marijke Heuff, GPL/John Glover, GPL/J S Sira; 181 top to bottom: GPL/Neil Holmes, GPL/Neil Holmes, GPL/John Glover, GPL/John Glover, GPL/J S Sira; 182 top to bottom: GPL/Neil Holmes, GPL/Howard Rice, Nicola Stocken Tomkins, GPL/Brian Carter, GPL/Brian Carter; 183 top to bottom: GPL/Neil Holmes, GPL/Howard Rice, GPL/Howard Rice, GPL/John Glover, GPL/Geoff Dann; 184 top to bottom: GPL/Clive Nichols. GPL/John Glover, GPL/Mark Bolton, GPL/Howard Rice, GPL/Eric Crichton; 185 top to bottom: GPL/John Glover, GPL/Howard Rice, GPL/John Glover, GPL/J S Sira, GPL/Mark Bolton; 186 top to bottom: GPL/Lamontagne, GPL/Brian Carter, GPL/Christopher Fairweather, GPL/Rex Butcher, GPL/Christopher Fairweather; 187 top to bottom: GPL/Neil Holmes, GPL/John Glover, GPL/Lamontagne, GPL/J S Sira, GPL/Neil Holmes 188 top to bottom: GPL/Brian Carter, GPL/Philippe Bonduel, GPL/John Glover, GPL/J S Sira, GPL/John Glover; 189 top to bottom: GPL/Neil Holmes, GPL/John Glover, GPL/Neil Holmes, GPL/Mayer/Le Scanff, GPL/Neil Holmes